— JANE —
AUSTEN
AND THE
ENGLISH
LANDSCAPE

JANE
AUSTEN
AND THE
ENGLISH
LANDSCAPE

MAVIS BATEY

BARN ELMS

FOR MY FAMILY

FIRST PUBLISHED IN 1996 BY
BARN ELMS PUBLISHING
93 CASTELNAU, LONDON SW13 9EL

PUBLISHED IN THE UNITED STATES BY
CHICAGO REVIEW PRESS, INC.
814 N. FRANKLIN STREET, CHICAGO, ILLINOIS, 60610

ORIGINATED BY YEO VALLEY GRAPHIC REPRODUCTION
PRINTED IN HONG KONG BY
MIDAS PRINTING LTD

DESIGN BY JESSICA SMITH

TEXT © MAVIS BATEY, 1996

ISBN 1-55652-306-8

_____

FRONTISPIECE: JANE AUSTEN DERIVED INSPIRATION FROM THE
LANDSCAPE AND COMFORTS OF SOUTHERN ENGLAND WITH ITS COUNTRY HOUSES,
PARKS, NESTLING VILLAGES AND FARMING LAND.

CONTENTS

CHAPTER ONE

THE

BACKGROUND

———

'TO SIT IN THE SHADE ON A
FINE DAY AND LOOK UPON VERDURE IS THE MOST
PERFECT REFRESHMENT', SAID FANNY PRICE
IN *MANSFIELD PARK*.

The eighteenth century was an age of stability and standardisation, but when Jane Austen wrote as it drew to its close various cross currents began to make their appearance in matters of 'Taste and Feeling'. We can follow these changes through the characters in her novels as she chronicles their attitudes and reactions with amused detachment. Her letters, with their minute social observation and lively awareness of the world around her, perfectly complement the novels.

The idea of linking sensibility and landscape in literature, art and landscape gardening had been gathering strength all through the eighteenth century and we can chart its progress in the sequence of Jane Austen's novels as the plots revolve around her heroines. Marianne Dashwood in *Sense and Sensibility* is a heroine whose excessive sensibility is derived from sentimental fiction; Catherine Morland of *Northanger Abbey* is a victim of a surfeit of gothic novels. Elizabeth Bennet of *Pride and Prejudice* loved walking in the countryside and country parks and, like her creator, was 'enamoured' of William Gilpin's writings on the Picturesque. The sober Fanny Price of *Mansfield Park* was an enthusiast for nature in the poet Cowper's mould and voices his concern about the fashion for professional landscape improvement. Emma Woodhouse, in *Emma*, has traditional values about the countryside and responsible landownership. Anne Elliot, in *Persuasion*, the most mature of the heroines, had to come to terms with the new romantic attitudes that prevailed when Jane Austen wrote her last novel in 1815.

Jane Austen began writing novels for the entertainment of her family and not in search of the fame they eventually brought her. Like Elizabeth Bennet, her favourite heroine, she had 'a lively, playful disposition, which delights in any thing ridiculous'. Unlike her sister author, Fanny Burney, she did not mingle with the social and literary world of her day. The materials she used were drawn from the world in which she moved and took delight, that 'little bit of ivory two inches wide' as she called it, on which she worked with 'so fine a brush' and such exquisite touch. Endings in her novels are always happy, there is no serious crime and any death that is mentioned has happened before the action of the novel begins. 'Let other pens dwell on guilt and misery' was how the author saw it.

Jane Austen only wrote about the things that were within the range of her imaginative inspiration – politics, life below stairs, the state of the economy, art connoisseurship and the like were wisely left for other novelists. It was all the more flattering for her to learn, in later years, that the Prince Regent was so delighted with her novels that he kept a set in each of his residences. He had indicated through his librarian that he would be graciously pleased to have her next novel, which proved to be *Emma*, dedicated to him. The prince's exotic lifestyle was a far cry from that of the Austens, but it is a measure of Jane Austen's talent that her novels should be

A WATERCOLOUR OF JANE AUSTEN
BY HER SISTER CASSANDRA PAINTED IN
1804, POSSIBLY AT LYME REGIS.
A RELATIVE WROTE; 'SHE HAD SUCH A
LOVE OF NATURAL SCENERY THAT SHE
WOULD SOMETIMES SAY THAT SHE
THOUGHT IT MUST FORM
ONE OF THE DELIGHTS
OF HEAVEN'.

JANE AUSTEN WAS FAMILIAR WITH BOX HILL, WHERE THE FAMOUS EXPLORING PARTY TOOK PLACE IN *EMMA*. MRS ELTON CALLED SURREY 'THE GARDEN OF ENGLAND', BUT EMMA THOUGHT THERE WERE OTHER CLAIMANTS TO THE TITLE, THE AUTHOR'S BROTHER'S COUNTY OF KENT BEING ONE OF THEM.

esteemed in the Brighton Pavilion as well as in the intimate circle of the Hampshire parsonage for which they were originally written.

The Austens were a lively, devoted and literary family who delighted in each other's company. The *Memoir*, written by Jane Austen's nephew, James Edward Austen-Leigh, talks of the stimulating atmosphere of her early days at Steventon rectory and 'the flow of native wit, with all the fun and nonsense of a large and clever family'. The family group was constantly changing and providing interest; James and Henry from Oxford and the younger sailor brothers Charles and Francis home on leave. Pupils of Mr Austen's stayed at the rectory and they had a wide circle of relatives and friends in the neighbourhood.

Reading novels out aloud together was a special pleasure, even amongst the more scholarly members of the family; extravagant, sentimental or would-be gothic incidents were parodied, charades enacted, scenes imagined and the sayings of favourite characters constantly quoted as part of their everyday conversation. The *Memoir* tells of Jane Austen's amazing familiarity with Samuel Richardson's *Sir Charles Grandison*, a family favourite; 'all that was ever said or done in the cedar parlour' was remembered and Jane would remind the family of Sir Charles's wedding anniversary on the appropriate day.

In her teens Jane Austen began to write herself, dedicating each piece appropriately to a special member of her extended family. These *Juvenilia* were largely burlesques of sentimental and gothic novels they had read and laughed at together. After Jane Austen came out and her horizons and contacts widened, her skill and confidence as a writer gradually matured as she shifted from literary to social satire. Her novels were now based on minute observation of the world around her; her father's parishioners, the houses of the Hampshire landowning gentry, assembly balls, visits to friends and relatives. 'That young lady has a talent for describing the involvements and feelings and characters of ordinary life, which is to me the most wonderful I have ever met with', wrote Sir Walter Scott with admiration when the novels were finally published.

Jane Austen's characters were never actually modelled on members of the family or neighbours; she was too clever an artist merely to imitate or caricature. The Bertrams, the Bennets, the Dashwoods are all pure invention, but into the novels are playfully woven, often as asides, the shared Austen experiences, reading and opinions which they had found entertaining; occasionally, endearing family habits and idiosyncrasies might be slipped in unobtrusively. The Austens could now involve themselves, not only with the actions of Sir Charles Grandison, Pamela, Evelina, Emmeline or Clarissa, but with the lives of their own Catherine Morland, Elinor and Marianne, Elizabeth Bennet and Mr Darcy.

Even when the novels were finally published the family still wanted to have more details and to continue the stories beyond the final chapter – the exact tip that Mrs Norris had given William in *Mansfield Park*; if Nancy Steele ever had a hope of catching Mr Davies in *Sense and Sensibility* or how long Mr Woodhouse lived to plague the newly-weds in *Emma*. Even though her novel later called *The Watsons* was never finished the family knew that Emma Watson would refuse a peer and marry a clergyman, a conclusion which met with their approval. Some of the family would have liked Fanny Price to marry Henry Crawford, who had more than a dash of their own lively, worldly-wise Henry about him.

Jane Austen's brother Edward was adopted as a young child by the Knights of Godmersham in Kent, which property he later inherited. One of his daughters re-called how her Aunt Jane would be sitting by the fire quietly at Godmersham and then would suddenly burst out laughing, jump up and run across the room to write something down at the desk before coming quietly back to resume her needlework. At her own home at Chawton, if unexpected visitors arrived she would push her manuscript under the blotter, and she refused to have the creaking door oiled, as it gave her due warning of their approach. Jane Austen called her sister Cassandra, with whom she shared a room, her 'other self'. Cassandra, three years the elder, did everything to protect and make life easier for the authoress. Jane was responsible for getting the breakfast, but Cassandra then spared her from all other household chores, so that she could get on with her writing. The protective, well-organised Cassandra was seen by later members of the family to represent 'the sense of Elinor' of *Sense and Sensibility*, although they saw none of Marianne's failings in Aunt Jane.

By the time the two sisters had put on their spinsters' caps, Fanny, their brother Edward's eldest daughter, appeared on the scene bringing with her all the freshness of the teenage world. Fanny came of age in 1811 and Jane Austen saw her as 'almost another sister'. She consulted Aunt Jane about her love affairs, knew the latest in fashion, played the harp and could talk about new dances and theatre. She revelled in discussing the characters and scenes in her aunt's novels, which brought much merriment to her father's drawing room and were also part of her own life.

If Jane Austen describes specific scenes in her novels they were always places with which she was acquainted or had read about, such as Bath, Box Hill, Blaise Castle, Portsmouth, Lyme Regis, the Peak district. She counselled another niece, her brother James's daughter, Anna, who aspired to novel writing, how important it was not to introduce unfamiliar local colour;

> Let the Portmans go to Ireland, but as you know nothing of the Manners there, you
> had better not go with them. You will be in danger of giving false representations.
> Stick to Bath and the Foresters. There you will be quite at home.

A CONTEMPORARY ENGRAVING OF FAMILY LIFE. WHEN THE AUSTEN FAMILY ASSEMBLED TOGETHER IN THE EVENING THEY TOOK PLEASURE IN READING NOVELS AND PASSAGES FROM COWPER AND DR JOHNSON ALOUD.

FANNY KNIGHT WITH HER
WATERCOLOURS PAINTED BY HER
AUNT CASSANDRA. 'YOU ARE THE DELIGHT
OF MY LIFE', JANE AUSTEN TOLD HER
NIECE, 'IT HAS BEEN VERY,
VERY GRATIFYING TO KNOW YOU
SO INTIMATELY'.

In a later letter to Anna, Jane Austen expressed her approval of the way her novel was shaping;

> You are now collecting your People delightfully, getting them exactly into such a spot as is the delight of my life; – 3 or 4 families in a Country Village is the very thing to work on.

Aunt Jane checked Anna's manuscript carefully with the family and told her that the journey from Bath to Dawlish should have taken two days; that Lyme was too far away to be talked of in Dawlish; that there was no title Desborough in the peerage and that her grandmother thought that one of the calls should have been returned sooner. Clearly the Austens had a trained eye for niceties and blunders in the writing of novels. Henry said that his sister wrote quickly but revised meticulously.

Jane Austen's comments to Anna reveal some of her own methods of writing; how she set her scenes geographically, with roadbook, almanac, guides and books of engravings to hand. Place names are chosen with care. Combe Magna, in *Sense and Sensibility*, sounds just right for Willoughby's home in the county of Somerset, as does the Woodhouses' Surrey village of Highbury in *Emma*, part of which Jane Austen wrote at her godfather's rectory at Great Bookham; her walks in the neighbourhood would have taken her through Norbury, Thornbury, Longbury, Maybury and Foxbury.

Distances between real places and the travelling time are always planned carefully, but this does not mean that the fictitious sites, such as Mansfield Park, Sanditon, Rosings or Sotherton, should be sought in the geographical place assigned to them. Having given Mansfield Park, in the first novel to be written with publication in mind, a location 'four miles from Northampton', everything is then made consistent. William and Fanny take the right time to get to and from Portsmouth and, after specific enquiries to her clerical family, Edmund is ordained at Peterborough in the right diocese. Mansfield Park itself, which has all the qualities of her brother's Godmersham and would be easily spotted by the family, can surely only have been placed in Northamptonshire to mislead readers.

Although it is the landscape of southern England which permeates her novels, the reason no country house or village is sited in her own county of Hampshire is to preserve the anonymity of the author and to avoid the possibility of giving offence to neighbours. It is in her mature novel *Emma*, published in 1816, that Jane Austen gives expression to her admiration of the landscape of the southern counties, 'sweet to the eye and mind, English verdure, English culture, English comfort', from which she derived such satisfaction and inspiration.

THE
FAMILIAR
RURAL SCENE

———

CHAWTON HOUSE. THE RURAL WALK
FROM THE VILLAGE ALONG THE GOSPORT ROAD
TO THE 'GREAT HOUSE' AND ROUND ITS PARKLAND
GAVE JANE AUSTEN MUCH PLEASURE AFTER THE
CONSTRAINTS OF BATH AND SOUTHAMPTON.

15

Jane Austen, the daughter of a Hampshire country parson, spent the first twenty-five formative years of her life in that county. The seventh child of a family of eight, she was born on 16 December 1775 at Steventon, about six miles west of Basingstoke. At an early age she started writing for the family and the first three of her novels were drafted at Steventon. Henry Austen gave the Revd George Austen the credit for fostering his sister's talent for writing, being, 'not only a profound scholar, but possessing a most exquisite taste in every species of literature'.

Mrs Austen had the reputation of combining a lively imagination and a practical nature. She was an energetic housekeeper and had no pretensions to grandeur, even though it was she who had the good family connections. She was proud of her dairy, brewhouse and poultry yard, and the family, who were enthusiastic gardeners, kept bees and had their own recipes for mead and currant wine; their strawberry beds were greatly admired by neighbours.

The Steventon rectory, just outside the village, was situated in the midst of good farming country and Mr Austen took charge of the productive glebe farm himself. William Gilpin dismissed the area on his picturesque tours and found 'little that excites attention' in such a rural landscape, but William Cobbett called it his favourite landscape for 'living in', and in his *Rural Rides* took pleasure in 'the size and the form of the fields, in the woods, the hedgerows, the sainfoin, the young wheat, the turnips, the tares, the fallows, the sheepfolds and the flocks'. This was the landscape of husbandry that delighted the Austens, not just as walkers, but with real involvement in the farming community. The whole family took a lively interest in ploughing matches, the state of the crops and the market price of their cattle. Mr Austen also held the living of Deane, a mile away, and although the parsonage was let to their friends, the Lloyds, he looked after the glebe farm there also.

The Lloyds were intimately connected with the Austens and two of the widowed Mrs Lloyd's daughters were to marry into the Austen family. Martha Lloyd joined the Austen household in 1806 after her mother's death and was a constant companion at Chawton, finally marrying Frank in 1828. The Lloyds had moved to Ibthorpe in 1792 when James took over the parsonage after his marriage to Anne Mathews; after only five years, however, Mary Lloyd returned to Deane parsonage, after Anne's death, as Mrs James Austen. Jane Austen had been most upset when the daily contact with Martha and Mary Lloyd had been broken in 1792, but there was consolation in being able to stay with them at Ibthorpe (which she always wrote as Ibthrop) in a part of Hampshire she grew to love. Ibthorpe was a hamlet of Hurstbourne Tarrant in the Hampshire highlands to the north-west of the county, which lies at the head of a narrow steep-sided valley watered by the little chalk Bourne stream; the rolling downs were an exhilarating contrast to the flatness of the

STEVENTON RECTORY DRAWN BY ANNA AUSTEN IN 1814. JANE AUSTEN SPENT THE FIRST 25 YEARS OF HER LIFE HERE.

countryside around Steventon. Jane Austen and Martha were, she said, 'desperate walkers' and out for hours on end in the fresh air of the downs.

Jane Austen began to write 'Elinor and Marianne', the first version of *Sense and Sensibility* in the mid 1790s, and there are echoes of her own delight in a downland landscape in the description of the countryside round Barton, which 'abounded in beautiful walks' and where 'the high downs' invited them from almost every window of the house 'to seek the exquisite enjoyment of air on their summits'. After they had 'gaily ascended the downs' Marianne exclaimed, with 'laughing delight' as she experienced the 'delightful sensations' of a high wind in her face, 'Is there a felicity in the world superior to this?' When the heavens opened there was the consolation of throwing propriety to the winds and rushing down the hill at top speed. There was no reported sprained ankle for Jane Austen at Ibthorpe in a similar situation and no Willoughby to pick her up, but there was an unmistakable autobiographical ring to Marianne's delight in running down the steep grassy hill with such abandon.

All the young energetic heroines of Jane Austen's early novels loved 'scampering about the country', as Miss Bingley scathingly commented after Elizabeth Bennet's three mile muddy dash to Netherfield to see her sister. Her 'crossing field after field at a quick pace, jumping over stiles, springing over puddles' had given her 'a face glowing with the warmth of exercise', which had obviously captivated Mr Darcy. Catherine Morland of *Northanger Abbey* also revelled in 'the pleasure of walking and breathing fresh air' and as a child 'loved nothing so well in the world as rolling down the green slope at the back of the house'; the family thought this must refer to the young Jane Austen herself and the grass slope behind the Steventon rectory.

The *Memoir* by Jane Austen's nephew describes the Steventon garden;

> North of the house, the road from Deane to Popham Lane ran at a sufficient distance from the front to allow a carriage drive, through turf and trees. On the south side the ground rose gently and was occupied by one of those old-fashioned gardens in which vegetables and flowers are combined, flanked and protected on the east by one of the thatched mud walls common in that country, and overshadowed by fine elms. Along the upper or southern side of their garden, ran a terrace of the finest turf.

The *Memoir* goes on to describe the type of double hedgerow that Jane Austen features in *Persuasion* where Anne Elliot inadvertently hears a conversation about herself carried on by Captain Wentworth and Louisa Musgrove in the concealed path near Uppercross. These hedgerows were much in evidence in the walks that Jane and Cassandra took between Steventon and their father's other church at Deane, a mile away, or when paying calls at the neighbouring houses of Manydown, Oakley and Ashe, or collecting the post from the Wheatsheaf Inn on the Winchester road.

A GLEBE MAP OF THE STEVENTON RECTORY SHOWING THE GARDEN WITH ITS ORNAMENTAL 'RUSTIC SHRUBBERY' FORMED FROM THE HEDGEROWS ROUND THE MEADOW. THIS FEATURE WAS TO BE REPEATED AT CHAWTON.

COTTAGES IN THE VILLAGE AT
IBTHORPE. JANE AUSTEN STAYED WITH
THE LLOYDS AT IBTHORPE HOUSE.

But the chief beauty of Steventon consisted in its hedgerows. A hedgerow, in that country, does not mean a thin formal line of quickset, but an irregular border of copse-wood and timber, often wide enough to contain within it a winding footpath, or a rough cart track.

The Steventon rectory garden had two such hedgerows radiating from it, which the Austens made into ornamental walks. According to the *Memoir* one, which was 'a continuation of the turf terrace, proceeded westward, forming the southern boundary of the home meadows; and was formed into a rustic shrubbery, with occasional seats, entitled "the Wood Walk".' The Austens were planning to improve their ornamental shrubberies by planting thorns and lilacs in front of the elm walk and to extend the orchard in the autumn of 1800, but by Christmas Jane Austen had learned, with horror, when she returned from a visit to Ibthorpe, that her father had decided to retire and take his family to live at Bath, where they would have no garden.

Characteristically, Jane Austen made the best of it, observing to her sister, 'It will be very pleasant to be near Sidney Gardens! We might go into the Labyrinth every day!' The Austens could not, in fact, have found anything nearer, as they settled on a house at 4 Bathwick Place, opposite Sydney Gardens. They enjoyed walking along the canal and making excursions around Bath, following Richard Warner's guide. Jane Austen already knew Bath well, having made several previous visits there with relatives. Like Catherine Morland of *Northanger Abbey* she had found it an

HAMPSHIRE WAS A
COUNTY OF TRACKS AND HEDGEROWS.

exciting place for a holiday; it was a different story, however, when like her more mature heroine, Anne Elliot in *Persuasion*, she was uprooted from her country home to live in the 'white glare' of Bath.

The year after Mr Austen's death in 1805 his widow and her daughters left Bath for a short stay in Clifton on the fringes of Bristol, with what Jane Austen described as 'happy feelings of escape'. They then went on a round of visiting relatives and returned in the autumn of 1806 to share lodgings with Frank and his wife in South-ampton, where they were joined by Martha Lloyd. Although the house there did have

a garden running back to the city wall with a gravel walk bordered by sweetbriar and roses and opportunities for fruit growing, its town situation did not provide the country walks and 'the sweets of housekeeping' in a village, which were so dear to Jane Austen and so conducive to her writing.

Through the happiest of circumstances a chance to return to rural Hampshire presented itself in 1809. Edward Austen, the second son, had had the good fortune to be adopted by relatives of his father, the wealthy, childless Knights, who owned Godmersham in Kent and Chawton in Hampshire as well as Steventon. Edward's career had been very different from that of his other brothers as he had made the Grand Tour and became a country landowner when he inherited the Knight properties in 1798. The steward's house at Chawton fell vacant in 1809 and was offered as a home to Mrs Austen. An additional attraction for the family was that, as patron of the living, Edward had settled his brother James in their old rectory home at Steventon, twelve miles away. Prose was inadequate to describe her feelings, so Jane Austen recorded them in verse for her sailor brother Francis.

> *As for ourselves, we're very well*
> *As unaffected prose will tell -*
> *Cassandra's pen will paint our state*
> *The many comforts that await*
> *Our Chawton home, how much we find*
> *Already in it, to our mind;*
> *And how convinced, that when complete*
> *It will all other Houses beat*
> *That ever have been made or mended*
> *With rooms concise, or rooms distended.*

It was with the greatest joy, after the six restless years of living in Bath and Southampton, that Jane Austen returned to the Hampshire scene. Having their own home and returning to the settled habits and duties of life in a country parish, walks in the countryside and the woods belonging to Edward's 'Great House', provided ideal conditions for the eight remaining years of Jane Austen's life. The countryside round Chawton with its beech woods, sheltered valleys, commons, hopfields, hollow lanes, hedgerows, downs and sheepwalks has been lovingly described by Gilbert White of the neighbouring parish of Selborne in *The Natural History and Antiquities of Selborne*. His book was a scientific and emotional response to Nature, admired by Coleridge as well as Darwin, and its 'nature calendar', with its daily record of birds, animals and plants in flower, must have been of great interest to the Austens. In 1776 White employed the Swiss-born artist Samuel Hieronymus Grimm at Selborne to 'take some of our finest views'.

SYDNEY GARDENS, BATH,

HAD TO COMPENSATE FOR THE

LACK OF A PRIVATE GARDEN

IN THE AUSTENS'

TOWN HOUSE.

Settled happily in such an environment, Jane Austen started to revise her early Steventon novels and to gather ideas for new ones. According to Cassandra, 'First Impressions', the original of *Pride and Prejudice*, was begun at Steventon in 1796; it had so impressed Mr Austen that the next year he wrote to Cadell the publisher to ask if they would like to see a manuscript three-volumed novel about the length of Fanny Burney's *Evelina*; the offer was declined. Jane Austen started on *Northanger Abbey* the following year and offered it to a publisher in 1803, but although ten pounds were paid for it, this too remained unpublished and only appeared after her death. As these publishing efforts had been so unsuccessful Jane Austen decided to pay for the costs herself. At Chawton the Austens no longer needed to pay for accommodation and their improved situation may have contributed to her decision to publish. Her brother Henry was now an associate in a banking firm and could advise her in financial matters. He also had a house in town, where she frequently stayed, and could give assistance over publishing contacts. When she was in London Jane Austen greatly enjoyed visiting theatres, exhibitions and fashionable shops.

Sense and Sensibility, originally begun in epistolary form as 'Elinor and Marianne', was the first of Jane Austen's novels to be revised; it was published 'for the author' in 1811. The circumstances of the widowed Mrs Dashwood, retiring with her daughters on £500 a year to a cottage on a relative's estate, were very similar to the Austens' own situation. So was the description of the cottage; 'as a house, Barton Cottage, though small, was comfortable and compact; but as a cottage it was defective, for the building was regular, the roof was tiled, the window shutters were not painted green, nor were the walls covered with honeysuckles'. The Austens' cottage was certainly no fashionable *cottage orné*, having been built in the reign of William and Mary and for a time used as an inn, but a concession was made to the playfulness that Regency architecture favoured when, as part of the alterations, Edward put in a new gothic window for his family on the garden side of the house.

Mansfield Park, written between 1811 and 1813, was the first new novel to take advantage of the tranquillity of Chawton, after the turmoil of Bath and Southampton.

We can hear Jane Austen speaking in Fanny Price, when, being forced to return to Portsmouth, she laments on losing all the pleasures of spring in the country;

> She had not known before what pleasures she had to lose in passing March and April in a town. She had not known before, how much the beginnings and progress of vegetation had delighted her. What admiration, both of body and mind, she had derived from watching the advance of that season which cannot, in spite of its capriciousness, be unlovely, and seeing its increasing beauties, from the earliest flowers, in the warmest divisions of her aunt's garden, to the opening of leaves of her uncle's plantation, and the glory of his woods.

When she returned to Mansfield Park and the countryside from Portsmouth, 'liberty, freshness, fragrance and verdure' came back into Fanny's life.

Fanny Price, like Jane Austen, was a devotee of William Cowper. She saw the countryside with Cowper's 'heart and eye' and with his love of simple rural pleasures. 'Scenes must be beautiful, which daily view'd, please daily', he had said, commending 'home-born happiness' and local attachment. Mr Austen used to read Cowper aloud in the evenings and Henry Austen's biographical notice of his sister said that, 'her favourite moral writers were Johnson in prose and Cowper in verse'. Fanny Price, like Jane Austen herself, loved to observe 'the appearance of the country, the bearings of the road, the difference of soil, the state of the harvest, the cottages, the cattle, the children', but Miss Crawford, who found happiness in the society of town, had none of Fanny's rural values or 'delicacy of taste, of mind, of feeling; she saw nature, inanimate nature with little observation'. Fanny Price in her rambling meditations brings to mind Cowper's lines from 'In the Shrubbery';

> *The saint or moralist should tread*
> *This moss-grown alley, musing, slow...*

When contemplating the shrubbery at the rectory she moralises about evergreens, memory and the amazing variety of Nature; 'One cannot fix one's eye on the commonest natural production without finding food for a rambling fancy', she muses. Miss Crawford, who was not, like Cowper or Fanny, particularly 'enamour'd of sequester'd scenes and charmed with rural beauty', was not impressed;

> 'To say the truth', she said wearily, 'I am something like the famous Doge at the court of Lewis XIV; and may declare that I see no wonder in this shrubbery equal to seeing myself in it. If anybody had told me a year ago that this place would be my home, that I should be spending month after month here, as I have done, I certainly should not have believed them.'

Cowper's theme of 'God made the country and man the town' dominates *Mansfield Park*. His long poem *The Task*, published in 1785, was written in his little

NEIGHBOURING SELBORNE, SEEN THROUGH THE TREES, WOULD HAVE BEEN FAMILIAR TO THE AUSTENS.

summerhouse at Olney, 'to discountenance the modern enthusiasm after a London life, and to recommend rural ease and leisure as friendly to the cause of piety and virtue'. His sentiment was endorsed by Mrs Austen, who after a short stay in London pronounced it 'a sad place, I could not live in it on any account; one has not time to do one's duty either to God or man'.

Fanny Price, like her creator, was only a cool romantic, but taking her cue from Cowper was an 'enthusiast for nature' and could rhapsodise about its sublimity with her feet on the ground. "'Here's harmony!' said she, 'Here's repose!',", as she looked out of the window on a moonlit night.

'When I look out on such a night as this, I feel as if there could be neither wickedness nor sorrow in the world; and there would certainly be less of both if the sublimity of Nature were more attended to, and people were carried more out of themselves by contemplating such a scene'.

Fanny had clearly been reading one of Cowper's letters recently published by William Hayley; 'Oh! I could spend whole days and moonlight nights in feeding upon a lovely prospect!' he wrote. 'If every human being upon earth could think for a quarter of an hour, as I have done for many years, there might be many miserable men among them, but not an unwakened one would be found'. In another letter he wrote;

I can look at the same rivulet or at a handsome tree every day of my life with new pleasure. This, indeed, is partly the effect of a natural taste for rural beauty and partly the effect of habit, for I never in all my life let slip the opportunity of breathing fresh air and of conversing with nature.

It was Cowper's poetry that inspired Jane Austen's generation with a love of gentle nature, which would later be overwhelmed by Wordsworth's 'mighty forces'. Marianne Dashwood, the romantic heroine of *Sense and Sensibility*, was still 'animated' by Cowper's 'beautiful lines'.

The publication of Cowper's letters for those who had loved his poetry was in itself a moving experience, but some years before, just after his death in 1800, there had appeared an unusual small book, *Cowper Illustrated by a Series of Views*, with engravings of the poet's haunts around his home in Olney to illustrate his verse. The rural scenery to the south-east of Northampton, round Olney and Weston Underwood, was described intimately in verse and letters through the eyes of the poet and it is interesting that Fanny's Cowper-like musings on Nature emanate from Mansfield Park, which we are told is four miles from Northampton. Cowper was very much in Fanny's mind when the implications of professional landscape improvements were discussed at Mansfield Park.

PORTRAIT OF THE POET WILLIAM COWPER. COWPER'S DESCRIPTION OF THE GENTLER ASPECTS OF NATURE AND RURAL PLEASURES STRUCK A CHORD WITH JANE AUSTEN.

COWPER'S SUMMER HOUSE AT
OLNEY SHOWN SURROUNDED BY
SHRUBBERY PLANTING

Cowper loved gardening, which solaced him during fits of depression, and gained much pleasure in walking in the Throckmortons' nearby garden at Weston Underwood. In *The Task* he described its shady walks and bowers, gothic temple in the wilderness, moss house in the shrubbery, groves, orchard, rustic bridge and avenue of lime trees, a 'monument of ancient taste'. Although a wilderness was originally a formal maze-like feature, it became a natural labyrinth in the eighteenth century, with walks bordered by trees and evergreens usually leading to garden buidings. In 1786 Cowper went to live in the lodge at Weston Underwood and was able to walk daily in its shrubberies and wilderness. It was the kind of garden that the Austens would have approved of and they would know, like the Bennets in *Pride and Prejudice*, that the winding walks of a wilderness gave 'ample space to narrow grounds' with 'deception innocent'.

The wilderness, shrubberies and orchards acted as outdoor rooms for confidential meetings in the plots in Jane Austen's novels and their own shrubbery walk at Chawton gave them the same pleasure as Cowper derived from his. In May 1811 Jane Austen wrote;

> Our young piony at the foot of the fir tree has just blown and looks very handsome, and the whole of the shrubbery border will soon be gay with pinks and sweet williams, in addition to the columbines already in bloom. The syringas too, are coming out.

She had said in Southampton; 'I could not do without a Syringa, for the sake of Cowper's line. We also talk of a laburnam'; it seems that syringa was also planted soon after they arrived at Chawton in Cowper's honour.

Cowper had described his shrubbery in detail in *The Task*; it contained as well as 'laburnum, rich in streaming gold' and 'syringa, iv'ry pure', roses, hollyhocks, guelder roses, lilac, hypericum, mezereon, broom and jasmine. The ingredients of the domestic happiness Cowper yearned for in his own life struck a chord in Jane Austen's heart.

> *Friends, books, a garden and perhaps his pen*
> *Delightful industry enjoyed at home.*

Her first requirement, however, amid the delights of rural pleasures was the companionship of her close-knit family.

BELOW LEFT: TWO ILLUSTRATIONS FROM COWPER ILLUSTRATED BY A SERIES OF VIEWS IN OR NEAR THE PARK OF WESTON UNDERWOOD, BUCKS.

CHAPTER THREE

THE
AGONIES
OF
SENSIBILITY

SIR BROOKE BOOTHBY AS AN '*ÂME SENSIBLE*'
LYING IN THE WOODS IN MELANCHOLY POSE READING ROUSSEAU.
BROOKE BOOTHBY BELONGED TO THE NUNEHAM SET WHO TRIED
TO INTERPRET ROUSSEAU FOR THE WORLD
OF FASHION.

We have Jane Austen's word for it that she started writing at the age of twelve. Her teenage works, the so-called *Juvenilia*, written between 1787 and 1793, were contained in three notebooks which she called, with mock pomp, Volume the First, Volume the Second and Volume the Third. They reflect well-held Austen opinions and common-sense values, particularly their dislike of sentimentality and soulful introspection. While up at Oxford, James Austen, who was a Fellow of St John's College, and his younger brother Henry Austen edited a journal called *The Loiterer*; it was launched in January 1789, just after Henry had arrived as a scholar at the college. Of the essays written before it ceased publication in March 1790, sixty were by James and twenty-seven by Henry Austen.

The journal, in Johnsonian prose, was anti-sentimental and anti-romantic and condemned that 'excess of sentiment and susceptibility which the works of the great Rousseau chiefly introduced, which every subsequent Novel has since foster'd and which the voluptuous manners of the present age but too eagerly embrace'. The Austen mentor, Dr Johnson, felt the same way about Rousseau's corrupting influence. 'Rousseau, Sir, is a very bad man', he thundered, 'I would rather sign a sentence for his transportation, than that of any felon who has gone from the Old Bailey these many years'.

Writing *The Loiterer* would have continued through the vacations at Steventon, much to the interest of the fourteen-year-old Jane Austen. An early piece in the journal, signed by one Sophia Sentiment, complains of the dullness of the paper to whose publication the writer had so eagerly been looking forward; it has a distinct ring of Jane Austen's youthful wit. In the manner in which Addison wrote in the *Spectator*, when he contributed mock pieces to himself, the young lady began; 'You must know, Sir, that I am a great reader, and not to mention some hundred volumes of novels and plays, have, in the two last summers, actually got through all the entertaining papers of our most celebrated writers including *The Spectator*'.

Whether or not the piece by Sophia Sentiment criticising *The Loiterer* was actually by the hand of Jane Austen, the latter had a better idea for exposing 'excess of sentiment and susceptibility' than through ponderous moral academic articles. She decided to try her hand at writing, for the amusement of the family, short burlesques of the sentimental novels which were then at the height of their popularity, replete with undying love, tyrannical parents, sacrificed daughters, suicides, catastrophes, bosom confidences, first impressions. The Austen family admitted to being 'great Novel-readers and not ashamed of being so', but approved of Charlotte Heywood in Jane Austen's *Sanditon*, who was 'sufficiently well-read in novels to supply her imagination and amusement but not at all unreasonably influenced by them'.

Love and Freindship was one of Jane Austen's first efforts to take up the

THE PARTING OF THE LOVERS IN ROUSSEAU'S *LA NOUVELLE HÉLOÏSE*.

THE FRONTISPIECE TO AN ENGLISH EDITION OF *THE SORROWS OF WERTHER*.

ROUSSEAU'S TOMB ON THE ISLAND AT
ERMENONVILLE, THE ENGLISH GARDEN
CREATED BY LORD HARCOURT'S FRIEND,
THE MARQUIS DE GIRARDIN. WOMEN WHO
MADE SENTIMENTAL PILGRIMAGES TO THE
SHRINE OF THE MAN OF NATURE CUT OFF
LOCKS OF THEIR HAIR AND BREAST-FED
THEIR BABIES IN FRONT OF HIS TOMB.

THIS ENGRAVING WOULD HAVE APPEALED
TO ROUSSEAU, BUT HIS CULT OF NOBLE
SAVAGERY WAS ANATHEMA TO THE
SELF-CONTROLLED AUSTENS.

precepts of *The Loiterer* and included a sentimental Sophia. Henry Austen in No.47 of *The Loiterer* had warned that all those who indulged in Rousseau's ideas and were 'tortured by the poignant delicacy of their own feelings' would inevitably 'fall martyrs to their own susceptibilities'. Laura in *Love and Freindship* was just such a Rousseau-addicted heroine with 'a sensibility too tremblingly alive to every affliction of my friends, my acquaintance and particularly to every affliction of my own'. Laura was also motivated by *The Sorrows of Werther* and she dismissed the agreeable, sensible Graham as soulless, because he had never read it. Undoubtedly the image of Sophia and her bosom friend Laura overcome by sensibility and fainting 'alternately on the sofa' would have delighted the assembled Austens and their friends.

Later in the year the editor of *The Loiterer* spoke of a 'lady who wanted to know whether he had read the Sorrows of Werther or the new Rousseau'. The lady who dubbed *La Nouvelle Héloïse* 'the new Rousseau' must surely have been his sister. Her *Lesley Castle* featured two sisters Charlotte and Eloisa. Goethe's Charlotte was the heroine and cause of the Sorrows of Werther, whose suicide after he discovered she was betrothed to his friend racked Europe. Jane Austen's Eloisa was cast in the mould of 'the new Rousseau', which had first opened the floodgates of sensibility. The Charlotte of *Frederica and Elfrida* accepted two suitors in one evening as she could not make anyone miserable, had a hearty supper and retired to bed; the next morning she was so overcome by guilt that 'she threw herself into a deep stream which ran thro' her aunt's pleasure grounds in Portland Place'.

Rousseau's message that we should abandon convention and listen to the dictates of our own hearts for guidance was, of course, anathema to the self-controlled Austens. *The Loiterer* forcibly argued that 'restraint and government contribute to happiness'. Rousseau's half-baked ideas on noble savages and the belief that only in the natural state could men be both good and happy was received with incredulity in the Austen household. Being natural by their standards was best expressed by Mr Knightley in *Emma* in reply to the silly Mrs Elton, who had suggested 'a sort of gypsy party' with 'everything as natural and simple as possible' for the strawberry picking gathering. 'My idea of the simple and the natural will be to have a table spread in the dining room', he said caustically. 'The nature and simplicity of ladies and gentlemen, with their servants and furniture, I think is best observed by meals within doors'.

Henry and James Austen must have regaled the Steventon family with the story of a Rousseauist who was well known in Oxford and so gave their sister the opening cue for her *Henry and Eliza* in 1789. Believing that her piece, unlike *The Loiterer*, would never appear in print, she felt free to use the actual name of the Rousseauist – George Harcourt. George Simon Harcourt succeeded to his father's estate at Nuneham Courtenay in 1777. He had been Rousseau's patron during his short exile in England and when the great Man of Feeling died in France he was sent his pocket

HUMPHRY REPTON PASTED THIS WATERCOLOUR INTO THE NUNEHAM GUIDEBOOK NEWLY WRITTEN BY LORD HARCOURT AND GIVEN TO HIM ON HIS VISIT IN 1798. IT SHOWS THE SENTIMENTAL URN DEDICATED TO VISCOUNTESS PALMERSTON IN 'FOREST LAWN' PLANTING.

LEFT AND ABOVE: LORD HARCOURT'S FLOWER GARDEN AT NUNEHAM COURTENAY.
THE DESIGN WAS BASED ON THE PRECEPTS OF JULIE'S ELYSÉE IN *LA NOUVELLE HÉLOÏSE*
AND HAD A WOODBINE BOWER, A TEMPLE OF FLORA AND
SENTIMENTAL URNS AND INSCRIPTIONS.

book, which had been the object closest to his heart at the moment he expired. This was kept at Nuneham in a special museum with other Rousseau relics. Lord Harcourt's Rousseauism caused much amusement, and his country seat, which was only five miles from Oxford along the Thames, was a favourite boating excursion for members of the university.

What seems to have taken Jane Austen's fancy was the account of the Nuneham feast, with Rousseau rewards for virtue and industry, which appeared in the *Annual Register* in August 1789. Lord and Lady Harcourt presented these awards after the haymaking, as Julie or La Nouvelle Héloïse had done on the Wolmar estate at a special Fête de Vertu on the lawns of the big house. To strike a real Rousseau note two pictures were erected on the lawn; one of a cottage with clean children and a busy housewife plying her wheel, which the villagers wreathed with roses, and a second showing a dirty cottage, uncared-for children and an idle housewife, which they had to wreathe with stinging nettles. During the year the Harcourts visited the homes of the busy, clean villagers and gave them red letter Ms for Merit to put in their windows and in their hats, but shunned the houses of the idle, dirty tenants.

Henry and Eliza begins: 'As Sir George and Lady Harcourt were superintending the labours of their haymakers, rewarding the industry of some by smiles of approbation, rewarding the idleness of others, by a cudgel...'. What would have delighted Jane Austen, if she could have known about it, is a poem buried in the Harcourt papers which pays tribute to Lady Harcourt's condescending welfare for the virtuous:

ILLUSTRATIONS FROM CHARLOTTE SMITH'S
ELEGIAC SONNETS

> *Here again my Lady stands*
> *Gives the prizes with her fair hands*
> *And with winning words between*
> *Bades then all be good and clean.*

A Rousseau garden on the lines of Julie's Elysée was created at Nuneham by William Mason, with a quotation from *La Nouvelle Héloïse* at the entrance. Everything grew naturally, 'without order or symmetry'; creepers twined from tree to tree, 'negligently as they do in the forest'; the path laced with Rousseau's favourite flower, the periwinkle, wound irregularly round the glade, 'like the steps of an indolent man', and in the wildest part a statue was erected to the true Man of Nature with an inscription by the Harcourts' cousin, Brooke Boothby, a fellow Rousseau addict:

> *Say is the heart to virtue warm?*
> *Can Genius animate the feeling breast?*
> *Approach, behold this venerable form*
> *T'is ROUSSEAU, let thy Bosom speak the rest!*

Rousseau told Brooke Boothby that he was delighted to hear that he had been given a memorial in Nuneham's Elysée.

*'BUT THE WILD GLOOMY SCENE HAS CHARMS FOR ME
AND SUITS THE MOURNFUL TEMPER OF MY SOUL'*

Sentimental objects, such as urns, bowers, altars of reverie and inscriptions appeared in pleasure grounds as part of the cult of pleasing melancholy. At Nuneham Mason erected a 'woodbine bower', such as the sentimental Nerina craved for in Book IV of his poem *The English Garden*. To make sure that the soul was raised to virtue through sensibility, Lord Harcourt placed sentimental inscriptions on urns commemorating dead friends, who 'living lov'd the haunts'. One such, dedicated to Viscountess Palmerston and written by the Poet Laureate, William Whitehead, read; 'O! if kind pity steal on virtue's eye/ Check not the tear, nor stop the useful sigh'. The earl wrote his own guidebook giving all the inscriptions so that visitors who came at dusk should not be deprived of the sentimental experience.

Bowers, summerhouses and arbours were favoured for meditation and reading in landscaped gardens. Even small Regency villas with enclosed gardens could have the sort of whimsical conceits read about in sentimental novels. The story of Camilla being trapped in the elevated summerhouse being built by Mr Dubster the shop-keeper, after her brother took the ladder away, greatly intrigued Fanny Burney's readers, including Jane Austen. In 1796, the year she was twenty-one, Mr Austen allowed his daughter to see her name in print by subscribing to *Camilla*. On the imposing subscription list was the entry: Miss J Austen, Steventon. A few weeks after Jane Austen had received the novel she was writing to her sister from Kent, having learned that she could not count on her brother's carriage for an immediate return trip; 'Tomorrow I shall be just like Camilla in Dubster's summer-house, for my Lionel will have taken away the ladder by which I came here'.

Jane Austen's own literary sentimental garden building was the focus for her *Catherine or the Bower*. The lonely, orphaned Catherine, who was brought up by an over-protective aunt, found solace in a bower at the end of a retired walk, which she had made herself as a child with the help of two young friends in the village; she was greatly distressed when they left the district and could only console herself with tender recollections of the pleasant hours they had spent together. Catherine soon became a great novel reader, however, and when a new companion, Camilla Stanley, came to join her in the bower she was eager to know whether their sentiments as to books were similar;

> 'You have read Mrs Smith's novels, I suppose?' said she to her companion. 'Oh! Yes, replied the other, I am quite delighted with them – They are the sweetest things in the world – 'And which do you prefer of them?' 'Oh! dear, I think there is no comparison between them – *Emmeline* is so much better than any of the others –'.

Mrs Charlotte Smith had the lead in sweet, heart-rending tales of distressed heroines; her own courageous life story was distressing enough to supply many of the incidents in her sentimental novels. She had lived happily at Bignor Park in Sussex, but when her father wished to remarry he arranged for the fifteen-year-old Charlotte to marry the dissolute Benjamin Smith by whom she had twelve children. She spent some time with him in a debtors' prison and when they finally separated had to bring up the remaining children on her own. She had started life as a poetess, greatly admiring Cowper, from whose poetry she said she 'derived infinite consolation'; she only turned to novel writing, which she regarded as inferior, to provide for her children. For a decade she wrote one four-volume novel a year. One of them, *The Old Manor House*, was begun at William Hayley's house at Eartham in Sussex when Cowper was staying there. In the evening Mrs Smith read aloud to the assembled company the chapter she had written during the day. Cowper wrote to his host on his return;

> I know not a more pitiable case. Chained to her desk like a slave to his oar, with no other means of subsistence for herself and her numerous children, with a broken con-stitution, unequal to the severe labour enjoined by necessity, she is indeed to be pitied.

Like her heroine Ethelinde, Charlotte Smith was a 'lady of sublime taste' who had learned to see 'the face of nature with the taste of a painter and the enthusiasm of a poet'. She was much influenced by Rousseau and Goethe's *Sorrows of Werther* and had been taught drawing by George Smith of Chichester. The Smith brothers of Chichester specialised in their own brand of sweet rustic picturesque by depicting in-timate scenes of pastoral Sussex with its downs, folded flocks, woods, ponds, cottages and apple-pickers, which predated William Gilpin's rugged picturesque of rocks, lakes and mountains in remote parts of Britain.

Charlotte Smith's 'sweet' novels were laced with poetry and her prose flows from it; 'dear delusions', 'spirit-wounding pangs', 'a bosom that bleeds with vain remorse and unextinguished love'. Remembering nostalgically her happy Sussex childhood she learned to link landscape and feeling; she wrote in a way which was, 'descriptive of the scene and the state of mind in which I surveyed it'.

By 1797 Jane Austen was ready to come to terms with the claims of sensibility, no longer in the form of the burlesque of her early writing but by presenting the two different attitudes to tribulations, the one through sense and the other through sensi-bility, and letting the message speak for itself. The story of the two sisters who faced their love dilemmas in different ways in her novel *Sense and Sensibility* was originally called 'Elinor and Marianne'. Like any of Charlotte Smith's heroines Marianne Dashwood suffered deep 'embosm'd grief' and 'indulgence of feeling'. As with Char-lotte Smith, it was Cowper who aroused Marianne's feelings and she was so critical of Edward Ferrars for his reading of Cowper's 'beautiful lines which have frequently

almost driven me wild, pronounced with such impenetrable calmness, such dreadful indifference' that she questioned her sister's choice of lover.

Mrs Dashwood thought Edward would have been seen in a better light if Marianne had given him simple prose and not Cowper's poetry to read, but Marianne was not prepared to acknowledge grey areas in matters of Feeling.

'Nay, Mama, if he is not to be animated by Cowper!... Elinor has not my feelings, and therefore she may overlook it, and be happy with him. But it would have broke my heart had I loved him, to hear him read with so little sensibility'.

Marianne and her family were, like Charlotte Smith, forced to leave their beloved Sussex home. 'Dear, dear Norland!' said Marianne, as she wandered alone before the house, on the last evening of their being there; 'when shall I cease to regret you! when learn to feel a home elsewhere!'

Charlotte Smith had written eloquently in her *Elegiac Sonnets* 'On leaving a part of Sussex'. '*My early vows were paid to Nature's shrine, / sighing I resign Thy solitary beauties*'. The melancholy in her mind was associated with autumn in the beloved county which had inspired her.

When latest Autumn spreads her evening veil
And the grey mists from these dim waves arise
I love to listen to the hollow sighs
Through the half leafless wood that breathes the gale
O Melancholy! – Such thy magic powers,
That to the soul these dreams are often sweet.
And soothe the pensive visionary mind!

Marianne recalls with equal fervour memories of autumn in Sussex when Edward visits the Dashwoods in their new home.

'Have you been lately in Sussex?' said Elinor,
'I was at Norland about a month ago'.
'And how does dear, dear Norland look?' cried Marianne.
'Dear, dear Norland', said Elinor, 'probably looks much as it always does at this time of the year. The woods and walks thickly covered with dead leaves'.
'Oh!' cried Marianne, 'with what transporting sensations have I formerly seen them fall! How have I delighted, as I walked, to see them driven in showers about me by the wind! What feelings have they, the season, the air altogether inspired! Now there is no one to regard them! They are seen only as a nuisance, swept hastily off, and driven as much as possible from the sight'.
'It is not every one', said Elinor, 'who has your passion for dead leaves'.

PREVIOUS PAGE: A CLASSICAL LANDSCAPE BY GEORGE SMITH OF CHICHESTER. GEORGE SMITH BROUGHT THE IMAGE OF CLAUDE'S GOLDEN AGE TO THE RUSTIC PICTURESQUE LANDSCAPE AROUND CHICHESTER, WHERE HE AND HIS PUPIL CHARLOTTE SMITH LIVED.

Elinor tries to console Colonel Brandon, who has heard Marianne's pronouncement against 'second attachments', that although at present 'her opinions are all romantic' a few years will settle them 'on the reasonable basis of common sense and observation; and then they may be more easy to define and to justify than they now are, by any body but herself'. Breaking with the tradition of sentimental novels, Marianne, after a broken heart, goes on to marry the colonel, who is 'on the wrong side of five and thirty' and had once complained of rheumatism.

Jane Austen's final chapter champions sense against excessive sensibility, exerting more influence on the follies of sentimental novels than her brothers' forgotten *Loiterer* could ever have done. *Sense and Sensibility* turns its back on love at first sight, tyrannical parents, suicidal tendencies and even romantic love itself.

> Marianne Dashwood was born to an extraordinary fate. She was born to discover the falsehood of her own opinions, and to counteract, by her conduct, her most favourite maxims. She was born to overcome an affection formed so late in life as at seventeen, and with no other sentiment superior to strong esteem and lively friendship, voluntarily to give her hand to another! and that other, a man who had suffered no less than herself under the event of a former attachment, whom, two years before, she had considered too old to be married, and who still sought the constitutional safeguard of a flannel waistcoat!

But so it was, and, unlike the heroine of a sentimental novel, at nineteen she submitted 'to new attachments, entering on new duties, placed in a new home, a wife, the mistress of a family and the patronage of a village'. Even the garden at Delaford was old-fashioned with shut-in walled gardens, a canal, dovecote and fishponds; there were no sentimental garden ornaments nor romantic bowers, but only an old yew arbour behind the house, from which the Brandons could observe the carriages going along the turnpike road a quarter of a mile away.

LEFT: THE HOP PICKERS, AN ENGRAVING AFTER GEORGE SMITH OF CHICHESTER OF AN AUTUMNAL SCENE IN SWEET SUSSEX.

THE

GOTHIC

IMAGINATION

———

THOMAS JONES'S *THE BARD*
REFLECTS POETIC SUBLIME HORROR
IN THE GOTHIC MOOD OF
THE LANDSCAPE.

The gothic and sentimental moods in literature, art, architecture and landscape gardening flourished side by side in the eighteenth century and were often so intricately interwoven as to be indistinguishable. Catherine of The Bower could revel in Charlotte Smith's novels – 'the sweetest things in the world' – at the same time as Catherine Morland in *Northanger Abbey* was eagerly pursuing the 'horrid' spine-chilling gothic novels of Mrs Radcliffe and others which had been recommended to her friend, Isabella, by a Miss Andrews, 'a sweet girl, one of the sweetest creatures in the world', who had read every one of them.

The Loiterer had attributed the cult of the sentimental, called by Dr Johnson, 'the fashionable whine of sensibility' to the publication of Rousseau's *Julie, ou La Nouvelle Héloïse* in 1761; the inspiration of the gothic novel came from much earlier poetic sources associated with melancholy, particularly Milton's *Il Penseroso*. Thomas Warton's *The Pleasures of Melancholy* in 1747 hinted at new possibilities of exploiting the gothic mood with such thoughts as, '*Beneath yon ruin'd abbey's moss-grown piles/ Oft let me sit, at twilight hour of Eve... Or let me tread its neighb'ring walk of pines*'.

O lead me, Queen Sublime, to solemn glooms
Congenial with my soul; to cheerless shades,
To ruin'd seats, to twilight cells and bowers.

The 'Graveyard Poets' of the time wrote melancholy works on the theme of human mortality. The longest of them, Edward Young's *Night Thoughts* of 1742, ran to 10,000 lines in nine books; Robert Blair's *The Grave*, celebrating the horrors of death, followed the next year. Gothic melancholy poets did indeed seek 'solemn glooms congenial with my soul', backed up by the Miltonic props of mossy cells, gloomy pines, hollow caves, dim religious light, ruins and the inevitable screech owls. Catherine Morland eagerly expected to find 'delightful melancholy' in the gloomy aspects of the fir grove at Northanger Abbey.

The Swiss experience, as encountered on the Grand Tour, brought sublimity into the realm of poetic landscape. 'Precipices, mountains, torrents, wolves, rumbling, Salvator Rosa', exclaimed the young Horace Walpole ecstatically. Gray's *The Bard*, published by Walpole's Strawberry Hill Press in 1757, with its scenery of caves and torrents, awful voices, giant oaks and affrighted ravens forecasting the doom of the Plantagenets, who had massacred the Welsh bards, gave further encouragement to the gothic mood. The letters of the celebrated Blue Stockings are full of references to horrid rocks and roaring torrents, scenes to 'raise the imagination to sublime enthusiasm and to soften the heart to poetic melancholy'.

The powerful Ossianic cult of primitive landscape moods followed in 1762, when James Macpherson claimed he had discovered a genuine Gaelic poem which took the Sublime to even headier heights;

SALVATOR ROSA'S WILD AND ROCKY LANDSCAPES WITH STORM-RENT TREES WERE AN INSPIRATION FOR THOSE SEEKING THE SUBLIME EXPERIENCE.

Weep on the rocks of roaring winds, O maid of Inistore! Bend thy fair head over the waves, thou lovelier than the ghost of the hills, when it moves, in a sun beam, at noon, over the silence of Morven! He is fallen! thy youth is low! pale beneath the sword of Cuthullin! No more shall valour raise thy love to match the blood of kings, Trenar, graceful Trenar, died, O maid of Inistore. His grey dogs are howling at home; they see his passing ghost. His bow is in the hall unstrung. No sound is in the hills of his hinds!

Ossian swept through Europe: Goethe was much affected by his great realm of Nature and quoted it at length in *Werther*. Even after its Gaelic authenticity had been called into question, Ossian's popularity continued and the work was one of Napoleon's favourites. Dr Johnson thought it was a fake from the beginning.

TWO OF WILLIAM BLAKE'S ILLUSTRATIONS FOR BLAIR'S *THE GRAVE*. BLAKE ADDED HIS OWN INTENSE MYSTIC VISION TO THE SUBJECT.

OVERLEAF: AN AVALANCHE IN THE ALPS, BY DE LOUTHERBOURG. THE SWISS EXPERIENCE ON THE GRAND TOUR GREATLY ENHANCED THE FEELING FOR THE SUBLIME.

Poetry had a very powerful effect on the laying out of gardens; indeed Joseph Warton's description of landscaped gardens was 'practical poetry'. Alexander Pope, as poet and gardener, had the strongest influence on poetic landscape, especially on the garden buildings. His heroic poem *Eloisa to Abelard* of 1717 placed the tragic Eloisa in a gothic Miltonic landscape with deep solitudes and awful cells, mould'ring towers, darksome pines, caverns and grots and twilight groves. Hermitages, towers, ruins, caverns and grottoes soon appeared even in the gardens of hunting squires. The first purpose-built ruin to ornament a landscape was Alfred's Hall at Cirencester

Park, designed by Pope and Lord Bathurst in 1721; they were delighted when ten years later it was taken for a genuine relic of Alfred's time by an antiquarian. Sanderson Miller went on to specialise in ruined castles, wherever possible 'embosm'd high in tufted trees' in the Milton manner.

Edmund Burke's *A Philosophical Enquiry into the Sublime and the Beautiful* (1757) added a new dimension to the cult of sublimity. The eighteenth century liked to have its taste and feeling sanctioned by philosophy and Burke was able to relate the new gothic passions to the Sublime and to reassure his readers that a certain amount of horror was good for them. The passion caused by the great and the Sublime in Nature was astonishment, he told them, and, 'whatever is terrible, or is conversant about terrible objects or operates in a manner analogous to terror is a source of the Sublime, that is, it is productive of the strongest emotion, which the mind is capable of feeling'. A nice Burkean touch was to suggest that scenes of terror had a beneficial purging effect by giving exercise and relief to some part of the brain otherwise congested by lack of exercise.

Landowners fortunate enough to have sublime scenery on their estates could exploit agreeable sensations related to horror in their landscaped gardens. Dr Johnson, who was no great admirer of landscape improvements, was much impressed with Hawkstone's Burkean effects and thought it would have merited being described by Milton himself. Johnson found that 'the awfulness of its shades, the horrors of its precipices, the verdure of its hollows, and the loftiness of its rocks; the ideas it forces upon the mind are sublime, the dreadful and the vast. Above is inaccessible altitude, below is horrible profundity'. The Awful Precipice takes its name from Dr Johnson's remarks. There is also a sublime Swiss experience, where a rustic bridge crosses a deep gulf, and as a climax there is a remarkable series of chambers and grottoes excavated from the sandstone, giving much scope for the imagination.

Thrilling sensations were to be followed by enhanced tranquillity for the contemplation of the Sublime. Mount Edgcumbe in Cornwall is a sea-girt landscaped garden and at one point a zig-zag path was cut into the cliffs down to the rocks below and called 'The Horrors'. James Forbes describes the powerful emotion when 'you hear the murmuring of the waves dashing against the rocks far below, without seeing anything of them'.

The Sublime was also harnessed in Wales by Thomas Johnes at Hafod. In his wild landscape, after the same requisite feeling of fear and suspense, 'safely arrived, no language can image out the sublimity of the scene; which without quite arriving at a sentiment of aversion, produces, in the empassioned soul, all those thrilling sensations of terror, which ever arise from majestical, yet gloomy exhibitions'; so wrote George Cumberland, author of *British Landscape* and friend of William Blake. At one point he exclaimed; 'in the language of Ossian, "when the blast has entered the womb of the mountain-cloud and scattered its curling gloom around", for here, on this globose promontory, a bard might indeed sit, and draw all his fine images from nature!'.

A real Ossianic site was to be found near Dunkeld, which served as winter quarters for the Dukes of Atholl and lay not far from the family seat at Blair Castle. Here, in 1783, the 4th Duke installed a painting of the ancient bard in the hermitage built by his father overlooking the spectacular Black Lynn Falls on the river Braan, known thereafter as Ossian's Hall. Here the 'ghost of the hills' could be evoked in the Gaelic landscape. William Gilpin admired the wild landscape but thought that it was spoilt by the elaborate hermitage. Wordsworth was outraged by the 'intrusive Pile' and thankfully 'recoiled into the wilderness'.

Further down the scale the two ladies of Llangollen lived in a gothic house with ruins and arches in the garden and a hermitage seat where they read Ossian together. One truly rustic hermitage which Jane Austen must have known was on the top of the zig-zag path on Selborne hanger, four miles away from Chawton, which had been built by Gilbert White, the naturalist, behind his house The Wakes, where he lived until 1793. His parson brother Henry occasionally dressed up as the hermit for the benefit of visitors. In *Pride and Prejudice* Mrs Bennet suggests that Elizabeth might show Lady Catherine de Bourgh their hermitage, but we have no details of how rustic or primitive it was as the furious Lady Catherine did not give it as much as a glance as she strode through the Longbourn garden. It is unlikely that Mr Bennet used it as a retreat even when his study was out of action.

In painting it was Fuseli who was the master of sublime terror promoted by the Graveyard Poets and Burke's philosophy. He portrayed dark human passions, subjects taken from Shakespeare, Milton and Ossian and added his own nightmare quality of supernatural horses alongside witches, goblins, ghosts and giants. He greatly influenced Goethe, who modelled Mephistopheles's horse on the one in *The Nightmare* of 1782. Fuseli had a great affinity with Blake and wrote the introduction to Blake's edition of Blair's *The Grave*. Both Blair's poem and Young's *Night Thoughts* were given greater intensity by Blake's visionary illustrations. Piranesi was another propagator of

BOTTOM: THE GOTHIC AND THE
SENTIMENTAL MERGE IN THIS PAINTING OF
A LAKE AND RUINED CHURCH BY
MOONLIGHT.

WALPOLE SAID HIS *CASTLE OF OTRANTO*
HAD BEEN INSPIRED BY
STRAWBERRY HILL

sublime terror with his popular engravings of dark vaulted dungeons, chained prisoners and instruments of torture.

The gothic novel inherited a tradition of emotional tension already well established in poetry, landscape gardening and painting. The theatre provided the extra dimension of shared gothic suspense. When John Home's *Douglas* with its overtones of Shakespeare's drama and Scottish balladry was first performed at Covent Garden in 1757, a London newspaper reported; 'Terror and pity reigned in every Breast till by Degrees the discovery is made, when a Tide of Joy breaks in upon us'. Tom Bertram, who was a prime mover in the *Mansfield Park* theatricals, boasted that he had acted out *Douglas*, 'every evening of my life through one Christmas holidays'. *Lovers' Vows*, a translation of Kotzebue's *Child of Love*, which the party daringly chose to act in Sir Thomas's absence, was full of such melodramatic tension.

Although the gothic novel flourished mainly in the 1790s, Horace Walpole had got it off to a good start when he published his spine-chilling *The Castle of Otranto, a Gothic Story* in 1764; its passion, drama and gothic superstition with a castle of horror, howling winds, bleeding statues, a praying skeleton, a gigantic hand in armour and Manfred stepping down from his portrait, took the country by storm. Walpole said it had been inspired by his own Strawberry Hill, but far from being horrid or threatening his little house was charming rococo gothic, quite unlike the overpowering neo-gothic castles that would follow in the next century.

Walpole was a romantic antiquarian, who wanted to breathe life into history. He had a lifelong love-affair with all things gothic; words like monastic, feudal, relics or chivalry were music to his ears. Strawberry Hill was only a modest little Twickenham house when he bought it in 1747, but he lost no time in converting it into a would-be gothic castle; the first one to be lived in, rather than just a folly. When a friend asked him if his garden was going to be gothic like his little castle, Walpole made it clear that he had no intention of emulating a gothic poet who would seek out 'the gloomiest shades as best suited to the pleasing melancholy that reigned in his mind', but wanted a garden for Strawberry Hill which would be 'nothing but riant and the gaiety of nature'.

Mrs Anne Radcliffe was the leading exponent of the gothic novel, which also relied on Burke's fear and suspense for its sublime effects. She revelled in horrifying adventures in remote haunted gothic castles in sublime landscapes. Her first novel, in 1789, *The Castles of Athlin and Dunbayne* was set in Scotland under the influence of Ossian. *A Sicilian Romance*, in 1790, was followed by *The Romance of the Forest* in 1791, *The Mysteries of Udolpho* in 1794 and *The Italian* in 1797. Mrs Radcliffe and her imitators were clearly manipulating taste in the circulating libraries. Poor Charlotte Smith, who was still slaving away to provide for her now grown-up but still poverty-stricken family, thought she would have to try her own hand at gothic novels to compete in the market. She complained, the year after *Udolpho*, in the preface to her second edition of *The Banished Man*;

> My ingenious contemporaries have so fully possessed themselves of every bastion and buttress of every gallery and gateway, together with all their furniture of ivy mantles and mossy battlements, owls, bats and ravens that I have hardly a watch tower, a Gothic arch, a cedar parlour, an illumined window to help myself to.

In 1798 Jane Austen embarked on her novel *Northanger Abbey*, when the gothic craze was still at its height. Its opening lines tell us; 'No one who had ever seen Catherine Morland in her infancy, would have supposed her born to be an heroine'. We are reassured that her mother did not die bringing her into the world and that her father was not addicted to locking up his daughters; although she started life plain, her looks improved by the time she was fifteen and for the next two years 'she was in training for a heroine'. Unlike Emmeline and all the other heroines of the time she was still not strikingly beautiful, although her complexion had improved, nor was she accomplished at music or drawing. However, as there was a singular dearth of heroes in the neighbourhood this did not matter greatly. Fortunately the unlikely heroine with such an unpromising start in life was taken to Bath and her adventures began when she was introduced by Isabella Thorpe to gothic novels. She was assured there was no lack of such hair-raising delights to be found in the Bath circulating libraries.

Isabella promised that when they had finished *The Mysteries of Udolpho*, which was giving Catherine such delightful horrors, they would read *The Italian* together and many others. 'I will read you their names directly', said Isabella, 'here they are in my pocket-book. Castle of Wolfenbach, Clermont, Mysterious Warnings, Necromancer of the Black Forest, Midnight Bell, Orphan of the Rhine, and Horrid Mysteries. Those will last us some time'. When Catherine replies, 'Yes, pretty well; but are they all horrid, are you sure they are all horrid?' the scene is set for Jane Austen to parody the follies of the misguided young heroine of *Northanger Abbey*.

There is an innocent enough start with her ignorance about landscape follies. When Blaise Castle was mentioned as a possible trip she immediately imagined 'an edifice like Udolpho'. Catherine's companions teased her into believing that it really was an old castle, the finest in England – worth going fifty miles to see with all the towers and long galleries she craved for. Blaise Castle had been erected in Thomas Farr's landscaped garden at Henbury in 1766 and there was nothing horrid about it; indeed it could easily have been lived in comfortably, as an estate worker later did. Farr was, however, a friend of Edmund Burke and he introduced the 'delicious terror' of the Sublime from local and invented legends; Giant Goram, robbers' caves and a Lovers' Leap, all of which Catherine would surely have enjoyed if the trip had not been cancelled.

JANE AUSTEN WOULD HAVE KNOWN THE HERMITAGE AT SELBORNE SHOWN HERE IN A PAINTING BY S.H.GRIMM, WITH HENRY WHITE AS THE HERMIT.

A WATERCOLOUR BY LADY LEIGHTON OF
THE GOTHIC SEAT AT PLAS NEWYDD
WHERE THE LADIES OF LLANGOLLEN WERE
WONT TO READ OSSIAN TOGETHER.

The Mysteries of Udolpho had taken over Catherine's waking moments. 'I should like to spend my whole life in reading it', she said ominously to Isabella. When the hero, Henry Tilney, appears and takes her up Beechen Cliff overlooking Bath with his sister, she compares the riverside walk hopefully with the South of France. He was surprised that she had been abroad, but it is soon explained that she was thinking of the country that Emily and her father travelled through in Udolpho. Catherine instantly apologises for mentioning it, as she feels sure that novels are not clever enough for gentlemen to read. The hero rises to the occasion;

> The person, be it gentleman or lady, who has not pleasure in a good novel, must be intolerably stupid. I have read all Mrs Radcliffe's works, and most of them with great pleasure. *The Mysteries of Udolpho*, when I had once begun it, I could not lay down again; I remember finishing it in two days - my hair standing on end the whole time.

Catherine was ecstatic when she was invited to stay at their Gloucestershire home, Northanger Abbey, by the Tilneys.

> Her passion for ancient edifices was next in degree to her passion for Henry Tilney – and castles and abbies made usually the charm of those reveries which his image did not fill. To see and explore the ramparts and keep of the one, or the cloisters of the other, had been for many weeks a darling wish... With all the chances against her of house, hall, place, park, court and cottage, Northanger turned up an abbey, and she was to be its inhabitant. Its long, damp passages, its narrow cells and ruined chapel, were to be within her daily reach, and she could not entirely subdue the hope of some traditional legends, some awful memorial of an injured and ill-fated nun.

Northanger Abbey proved to be no such edifice; it was all elegance and comfort and only the exterior court with the offices showed any signs of its conventual past. When the wind started to howl in her bedroom, however, like Adeline in *The Romance of the Forest*, Catherine was overcome by excitement when she found an old piece of paper in a chest; but this was no ancient deed and turned out to be a laundry list. Undaunted by this setback for a gothic heroine, however, it was not long before Catherine became suspicious of General Tilney's strange behaviour and Montoni attitudes and imagined that he had walled up his wife in a disused part of the abbey. When she was shown by his son how stupid her Radcliffean imagining had been she was overcome by confusion and forced to admit ruefully;

> Charming as were all Mrs Radcliffe's works and charming even those of her imitators, it was perhaps not in them that human nature, at least in the midland counties of England was to be looked for. Of the Alps and the Pyrenees, with their pine forests and their vices, they might give a faithful delineation; and Italy, Switzerland, and the

GILLRAY'S CARTOON OF LADIES READING 'MONK' LEWIS. DEPRAVITY WAS ADDED TO GOTHIC HORROR BY 'MONK' LEWIS AND SOMETHING 'UNCOMMONLY DREADFUL' IS HINTED AT IN *NORTHANGER ABBEY*.

BLAISE CASTLE, NEAR BRISTOL, WAS A DELIGHTFUL LANDSCAPE FOLLY. CATHERINE MORLAND WAS TEASED INTO IMAGINING IT AS A GOTHIC CASTLE LIKE UDOLPHO.

South of France, might be as fruitful in horrors as they were there represented. Catherine dare not doubt beyond her own country, and even of that, if hard pressed, would have yielded to northern and western extremities. But in the central part of England there was surely some security.

There was worse to come in the way of novels, as was hinted at in *Northanger Abbey*, depravity added to gothic horror with devastating results. John Thorpe, Isabella's wrong-minded brother, confesses that he has just read Matthew Gregory Lewis's *The Monk* at Oxford; this book with such scenes as a rape in a charnel house would, presumably, not have been read at Steventon. Catherine, when she is with the Tilneys up Beechen Cliff, announces that she has heard that something 'uncommonly dreadful' – 'more horrible than anything we have met with yet' is expected soon from London. 'Monk' Lewis's gothic verse *Tales of Wonder* duly appeared in 1801 and the female reaction to it is splendidly caricatured by Gillray.

The end was in sight for the gothic novel when Walter Scott's *Waverley* was published in 1814. In its preface he said that if he added to the title 'A Tale of other Days' every novel reader would have anticipated another Udolpho,

> of which the eastern wing has long been uninhabited, and the keys lost, or consigned to the care of some aged butler or housekeeper, whose trembling steps, about the middle of the second volume, were doomed to guide the hero or heroine to the ruinous precincts? Would not the owl have shrieked and the cricket cried on my very title-page?

Scott wrote true romantic historical novels with well researched authentic backgrounds. There would be no more fantasy Udolphos and no more fictitious ruins in landscaped gardens. Nothing less than seeing 'fair Melrose aright' by 'pale moon-light' would satisfy those in search of the romantic thrill of the gothic past.

Jane Austen was in difficulties. *Northanger Abbey* had remained with the publisher since 1803 and was still not published when *Waverley* appeared in 1814. The whole thrust of the novel had been the effect of gothic novels on a young heroine, and this theme could not be drastically changed. In her new preface she felt obliged to apologise that 'manners, books and opinions' had changed since she wrote her novel. The story of Catherine Morland and her out-dated gothic addictions was finally published posthumously in 1818.

ENAMOURED
OF GILPIN
ON THE
PICTURESQUE

———

KIRKSTALL ABBEY BY THOMAS GIRTIN.
THE DISCOVERY OF BRITAIN WAS A BY-PRODUCT OF THE
PICTURESQUE MOVEMENT. WATERCOLOUR PROVED TO BE
A PECULIARLY APPROPRIATE MEDIUM FOR PAINTING
OUTDOOR SCENES.

The gothic imagination often merged into the picturesque at the end of the eighteenth century, but, whereas the gothic had a literary origin, the picturesque, as the name implies, derived from a painterly concept. The pioneer of the Picturesque movement was the Revd William Gilpin, vicar of Boldre in the New Forest, whose creed exerted a strong influence on Jane Austen's generation growing up in the 1780s. His published Tours to picturesque parts of Britain were sought after by every person of taste who became eager to draw, collect prints and take part in the Discovery of Britain. In the preface to his Lakes Tour Gilpin expresses the hope that his work would not be considered 'inconsistent with the profession of a clergyman'.

Jane Austen's father and her brother James were naturally interested in the writings of a fellow Hampshire clergyman. Gilpin's modesty and down-to-earth writing would have endeared him to the Austens. Henry Austen said that his sister was 'from a very early age enamoured of Gilpin on the Picturesque' and no doubt, in the words of her Mr Collins in connection with his own leisure pursuits, she would have found these picturesque travel writings, 'a very innocent diversion, and perfectly compatible with the profession of a clergyman'.

Gilpin's first thoughts on the Picturesque were brought together while he was still a schoolmaster at Cheam and they developed from his suggestion that a student should cultivate a 'picture-making faculty' when reading descriptive passages in the classics. In 1768 he published an *Essay on Prints*, the first standard guide on the subject, for the instruction of the new large public for whom cheap prints had become available. He showed how to apply the principles of painting to the examination of prints to enable the layman to appreciate such matters as 'design, disposition, keeping and the distribution of light'.

From cultivating a picture imagination when reading and studying and evaluating prints, it was but a short step for Gilpin to suggest that the traveller should use the same faculty in viewing real landscape. In the Cheam school holidays he set forth 'in search of picturesque beauty' and, usually in school notebooks, recorded with descriptions and 'on-the-spot' sketches what he found to be 'pencil-provoking' first in the Wye, then in the Lakes, the Highlands and other rugged picturesque regions. Although these journeys were made in the 1770s, it was not until after he had left Cheam and settled in Hampshire that he was persuaded by his friends, Horace Walpole and William Mason, to publish his Picturesque Tours. They were immediately popular. The first edition of the Lakes Tour, in 1786, was sold out in a few days.

Gilpin gave a new meaning to the word scenery when he applied it to landscape; hitherto it had only related to stage scenery. His association of pictures with appreciation of natural scenery became the new craze of picturesque observation which was perfectly described by Jane Austen in *Northanger Abbey*, where the

AN ILLUSTRATION FROM '*GILPIN'S DAY*'. 'A PLEASING ARRANGEMENT OF IDEAS TAKEN FROM THE GENERAL FACE OF THE COUNTRY'. MANY TOURISTS COMPLAINED THAT THEY COULD NOT ACTUALLY IDENTIFY SUCH A LAKELAND SCENE.

fashionable Henry Tilney and his sister were seen to be 'viewing the country with the eyes of persons accustomed to drawing and decided on its capability of being formed into pictures with all the eagerness of real taste'. There is clear evidence that Jane Austen had read Gilpin's publications with interest and profit.

Henry Austen said of his sister that she was a 'warm and judicious admirer of landscape both in nature and on canvass' and 'in earlier days' she 'evinced great power of hand in the management of the pencil'. Perhaps, however, like Emma, who tried her hand at every form of drawing including landscapes, Jane Austen was 'not much deceived as to her own skill' as an artist. It was her brother James, a great lover of natural scenery, an admirer of Gilpin and a poet, who was said to have 'influenced her taste'. It was he who had written most of the anti-Rousseau essays in *The Loiterer*, which had sparked off his sister's early burlesques on sentimental novels. Gilpin's picturesque sensibility, stressing the visual qualities of Nature, was a convenient antidote to Rousseau's sentimental approach. Taste came down from the top, whereas feeling was individual and spontaneous and to Dr Johnson's followers, including the Steventon family, was suspect.

The cult of the Picturesque, so understandably defined by Gilpin, could be as-similated into eighteenth-century canons of collective taste, which Rousseau's ideas had challenged; it also widened the scope of aristocratic taste as even minor gentry and tradesmen who could not aspire to the Grand Tour or to making art collections could afford prints and the Home Tour. Fortunately, roads to out-of-the way parts of Britain had greatly improved, and, in any case, the Grand Tour and the Swiss experience had been halted by unrest in Europe.

The youthful Jane Austen had an opportunity to hint at this democratic devel-opment in her *Henry and Eliza*, written in 1789, where she mentioned Lord Harcourt, who was Rousseau's patron. The Highlands Tour had been published that year and she would have seen that it was dedicated to this same Lord Harcourt, who was also Gilpin's patron. In a comic linking of his Rousseauist romantic benevolence and pic-turesque addiction, she makes Lord Harcourt stop his carriage at a scenic spot 'to give the postilion an opportunity of admiring the beauty of the prospect'.

The sensible Augusta in *Love and Freindship* 'having a considerable taste for the beauties of nature, her curiosity to behold the delightful scenes it exhibited in that part of the world had been so much raised by Gilpin's Tour to the Highlands, that she had prevailed on her father to undertake a tour to Scotland'. In *Lesley Castle* Jane Austen describes the newly-married, London-based Lady Lesley's reaction to the first sight of her Scottish home, an 'old and mouldering castle' which was 'perched up on a Rock to appearance so totally inaccessible that I expected to be pulled up by a rope'. Gilpin's Scottish Tour fuelled Jane Austen's imagination with illustrations of such picturesque gothic castles.

Brought up at Scaleby Castle on the Borders and taught to draw by a gifted father, who was garrisoned at Carlisle Castle, Gilpin was always stirred by castles, border warfare and picturesque banditti in rugged wild scenery. He favoured shat-tered, ruined structures, not only for their rugged quality, but because the 'lightness of parts' allowed the landscape to be seen through the chasms. Farnham Castle was much too regular and he thought it would be more picturesque if a mallet were taken to it; he even thought that parts of Tintern Abbey would be improved by similar

CLAUDE LORRAIN: *HAGAR AND ANGEL*. GILPIN BROKE THE SPELL OF ITALIAN LANDSCAPE PAINTING BY SHOWING THAT BRITAIN WAS PICTURESQUE OR 'WORTHY OF PAINTING'.

treatment. Mrs Radcliffe found Gilpin's picturesque eye invaluable for descriptions; 'the gothic window is hung with festoons of ivy; the arch with pendent wreaths streaming from each broken coigne', he wrote. Gilpin, always speaking as a picturesque connoisseur, wished to give credit where credit was due for these British ruins so evocatively 'naturalized to the soil'. In his Northern Tour he wrote;

> What share of picturesque genius Cromwell might have, I know not. Certain however it is, that no man since Henry VIII has contributed more to adorn this country with picturesque ruins. The difference between the two masters lay chiefly in the style of ruins in which they composed. Henry adorned his landscapes with the ruins of abbeys. Cromwell with those of castles.

Jane Austen was obviously highly entertained by Gilpin's remarks and in her youthful *History of England* she volunteered the information under the entry on Henry VIII;

> The crimes and cruelties of this prince were too numerous to be mentioned and nothing can be said in his vindication, but that his abolishing religious houses and leaving them to be ruinous depredations of time has been of infinite use to the landscape of England in general.

Jane Austen was already well acquainted with one of Henry's picturesque compositions, as at the age of nine she attended a school in Reading which had a ruined abbey in the grounds. Gilpin had pointed to the ruined abbey as exclusively British. 'When popery prevails,' he said, 'the abbey is still entire and inhabited and of course less adapted to landscape'. Other peculiarly picturesque British assets to spur on the landscape painter were verdure, parks, ancient oaks, mists and cloudy skies. As yet there was no British School of landscape painting and it was the Italian Campagna scenery, painted by Claude and Poussin and seen on the Grand Tour, which infatuated Dilettanti patrons. Gilpin helped to break the spell of 'Italian light on English walls' and increasingly Britain was seen to be picturesque or 'worthy of painting' in terms of landscape rather than being simply a subject for mere antiquarian or topographical representations.

The more subtle medium of watercolour was found to be peculiarly adapted to homebred scenery, and the new portable watercolour box was a great asset to travellers for on-the-spot paintings. A Society of Painters in Water Colours was formed and frequent exhibitions of their work were held. One visitor wrote enthusiastically in 1808 that such exhibitions gave the spectator the same rewarding experience as a picturesque tour to the North; 'Mountains and cataracts, rivers, lakes and woods, deep romantic glens and sublime sweeps of country, engage the eye in endless and ever-varying succession'. Jane Austen was taken to a 'watercoloured Exhibition' in Spring Gardens in May 1813, when she was visiting Henry in London.

GILPIN WOULD HAVE PREFERRED TINTERN ABBEY TO DISPLAY EVEN MORE 'LIGHTNESS OF PARTS'.

CASSANDRA'S VERSION OF HENRY VIII IN HER SISTER'S *HISTORY OF ENGLAND*.

Gilpin's picturesque analysis of the varied scenery of different parts of Britain gave home tourists a new concept of regionalism. The early tourists had only looked for curiosities but picturesque travellers were shown how to analyse and see how 'variously Nature works up the scenery' in different regions; for instance, when touring the Wye the traveller must take note of 'the steepness of its bank, its mazy courses, the grounds, woods and rocks which are its native ornaments and the buildings which still further adorn its course'.

Gilpin made 'on-the-spot' sketches of details but the picturesque illustrations he worked up for his published Tours were not always topographically correct but based on an accurate analysis of the character of the region, rearranged to suit his picturesque principles. Although these were, as he said, 'a pleasing arrangement of ideas taken from the general face of the country', many tourists complained that they could not identify the spots they were supposed to find in his Tours.

William Combe made fun of the schoolmaster-clergyman in his *The Tour of Dr Syntax in Search of the Picturesque* in 1812;

> *Thus, tho' from truth I haply err,*
> *The scene preserve its character.*
> *What man of taste my right will doubt,*
> *To put things in, or leave things out.*

Jane Austen, who also saw the comical side of the Picturesque, was clearly intrigued with Rowlandson's illustrations and wrote to her sister from town; 'I have seen nobody in London yet with such a long chin as Dr Syntax'.

Gilpin's advice to amateur artists was straightforward and down-to-earth in terms of composition; foreground, middle distance and background; perspective by means of side-screens; attention to light and shade and grouping; the picturesque viewpoint was not panoramic but the preferred 'station' was somewhere half way up the hill; mists were more atmospheric than blue skies and were also useful for concealing parts you did not want to draw. Figures were also useful in the landscape, not only to give an idea of scale but for 'distinguishing roads from rivers'. He also maintained that; 'We must ever recollect that Nature is most defective in composition and must be a little assisted', and the artist was at liberty to do his own planting;

> Trees he may generally plant, or remove at pleasure. If a withered stump suit the form
> of his landscape better than a spreading oak, which he finds in nature, he may make
> the exchange – or he may make it, if he wish for a spreading oak, where he finds a
> withered trunk.

When Henry Tilney in *Northanger Abbey* delivered his 'lecture on the picturesque' to Catherine Morland up Beechen Cliff he adapted Gilpin's straightforward approach. Catherine found the Picturesque confusing; 'It seemed as if a good view were no longer to be taken from the top of an high hill, and that a clear blue sky was no longer a proof of a fine day', but, with her tongue in her cheek, Jane Austen tells us that Henry's instructions to Catherine were;

> so clear that she soon began to see beauty in everything admired by him, and her
> attention was so earnest, that he became perfectly satisfied of her having a great deal
> of natural taste. He talked of fore-grounds, distances, and second distances – side-
> screens and perspectives – lights and shades; and Catherine was so hopeful a scholar,
> that when they gained the top of Beechen Cliff, she voluntarily rejected the whole city
> of Bath, as unworthy to make part of a landscape.

One of Rowlandson's illustrations for *The Tour of Dr Syntax*.
William Combe satirised the Picturesque with its rugged objects and abrupt
deviations including the lean horse and pointed chin;

In my poor beast, as well as me,

A fine example you may see,

She's so abrupt in all her parts,

She's quite a subject for the arts.

Jane Austen, although a devotee of Gilpin, also saw that the
Picturesque had its comical side.

Gilpin had assured them in his Wye Tour that 'at Bath the buildings are strikingly splendid: but the picturesque eye finds little of amusement among such objects'. Having arrived at the top of the hill, Henry, with a wave of the hand, tried to assist Nature *à la* Gilpin and to remedy her foreground planting deficiencies by adorning the summit with a rocky fragment and a withered oak. Thereafter if Henry were not by her side, Catherine was afraid that 'she should not know what was picturesque when she saw it'.

Gilpin and picturesque theory also figure prominently in *Sense and Sensibility*. Marianne Dashwood is dismayed that, in addition to his insensitivity over reading Cowper's poetry, Edward Ferrars is apparently ignorant on the subject of the Picturesque when she starts to question him about the Devonshire landscape around Barton.

'I shall call hills steep, which ought to be bold; surfaces strange and uncouth, which ought to be irregular and rugged; and distant objects out of sight, which ought only to be indistinct through the soft medium of a hazy atmosphere', he said, 'It exactly answers my idea of a fine country, because it unites beauty and utility – and I dare say it is a picturesque one too, because you admire it; I can easily believe it to be full of rocks and promontories, grey moss and brush wood, but these are all lost on me. I know nothing of the picturesque'.

LEFT AND RIGHT: TWO ILLUSTRATIONS OF MOUNTAIN COUNTRY BY GILPIN. SUCH CASTLES FUELLED JANE AUSTEN'S IMAGINATION FOR HER YOUTHFUL 'LESLEY CASTLE'. EDWARD FERRARS WAS CLEAR THAT HAPPY VILLAGERS PLEASED HIM BETTER THAN 'THE FINEST BANDITTI IN THE WORLD'

In the ensuing discussion with Edward and her sister Elinor, Marianne concedes that the language describing the 'admiration of landscape scenery' has been 'hackneyed out of all sense and meaning' and that 'everybody pretends to feel and tries to describe with the taste and elegance of him who first described what picturesque beauty was'. In 1794 two Herefordshire squires Uvedale Price and Richard Payne Knight had sought to make an abstract theory from Gilpin's practical ideas and invented the concept of 'picturesqueness'. Knight maintained that this was a matter of association, conditioned by painters, but Price tried to make the Picturesque a separate abstract category comprising all rugged objects and abrupt deviations as Burke had categorised the philosophical components of the Beautiful and the Sublime. Gilpin, followed by Jane Austen and Marianne, confused the philosophical issue by continuing to refer to the hybrid 'picturesque beauty'.

ACKERMANN'S REPOSITORY OF ARTS IN THE STRAND. THE PICTURESQUE FOSTERED A GREAT CRAZE FOR COLLECTING PRINTS, WHICH WERE AFFORDABLE EVEN BY ELINOR DASHWOOD ON HER LIMITED ALLOWANCE.

Uvedale Price promulgated his ideas in his *Essay on the Picturesque* in 1794; it is doubtful whether the youthful Jane Austen read it at the time as *The Mysteries of Udolpho* appeared that year and would be filling her thoughts. Whether she ever wanted to read it one cannot know, but clearly one product of the picturesque controversy had not escaped her attention. After Knight had challenged Price's ideas, Price counter-attacked in 1801 with a *Dialogue on the Distinct Characters of the Picturesque and the Beautiful* in which Knight appears as Mr Howard, Price himself as Mr Hamilton, and, as a punchbag, there is a Mr Seymour, who knows nothing about the Picturesque.

Mr Seymour is mystified by the way the two picturesque connoisseurs on their walk enthuse about a hovel under a gnarled oak, a rude cottage, brushwood and exposed roots of trees, heath, gypsies in the shadows, broken ground and a rusty donkey. Mr Howard, alias Knight, explains that the appreciation of these rugged ideas has been learned from painters but his companion assures him that this appreciation comes intrinsically from the objects themselves. Either way, Mr Seymour is still inclined to think picturesque objects are useless and plain ugly. What a gift for Jane Austen to make the matter-of-fact Edward Ferrars pronounce against the rugged paraphernalia of the Picturesque;

> 'I like a fine prospect, but not on picturesque principles. I do not like crooked, blasted trees. I admire them much more if they are tall, straight and flourishing. I do not like ruins and tattered cottages. I am not fond of nettles, or heath blossoms. I have more pleasure in a snug farmhouse than a watch-tower and a troop of tidy, happy villagers please me better than the finest banditti in the world'.

Marianne looked 'with amazement at Edward, with compassion at her sister'. Elinor only laughed.

A strong autobiographical note can be detected in *Sense and Sensibility* and the two sisters Marianne and Elinor. Although it is Marianne the younger who, according to Edward, 'would have every book that tells her how to admire an old twisted tree' (as Gilpin had done in his *Forest Scenery*), it is Elinor who likes to collect 'every new print of merit' and is an amateur artist whose work was much admired. Marianne played the piano. It was the same in the Austen household where Cassandra was the artist and her sister was the pianist. When the Dashwoods settled in their cottage the first requirement had been to accommodate the piano and affix Elinor's drawings to the walls; the Austens had to make the same arrangements for Jane's piano and Cassandra's drawings when they settled into their new Chawton cottage.

Sense and Sensibility was the first novel to be revised at Chawton, followed soon afterwards by the new *Pride and Prejudice* in which the heroine had made a

picturesque tour. Elizabeth Bennet was clearly made to study Gilpin's Tour of the Lakes before she set off with the Gardiners 'in pursuit of novelty and amusement', Gilpin's own definition of picturesque travel.

> 'And when we do return, it shall not be like other travellers, without being able to give an accurate idea of any thing' she said, 'We will know where we have gone – we will recollect what we have seen. Lakes, mountains, and rivers shall not be jumbled together in our imaginations; nor, when we attempt to describe any particular scene, will we begin quarrelling about its relative situation'.

Jane Austen would clearly have loved to go on the Lakes tour, as her lucky brother Edward had done with the Knight family. There is no doubt, however, that she had read Gilpin's Lake Tour thoroughly as she picks up his instructions for the picturesque grouping of cows, which practically every landscape painter, including the young Turner, was subsequently to follow. In the second volume of his Tour Gilpin had advised that the only way to make cows group well was 'to unite three and remove the fourth' to a detached position. In *Pride and Prejudice* when Miss Bingley and Mrs Hurst, who have been less than civil to Elizabeth Bennet, are walking with

DOWNTON CASTLE, HEREFORDSHIRE, THE HOME OF RICHARD PAYNE KNIGHT, THE PICTURESQUE THEORETICIAN, AND THE SUBJECT OF HIS POEM *THE LANDSCAPE*. THIS WATERCOLOUR IS BY GILPIN'S NEPHEW, W.S.GILPIN.

Mr Darcy in the Netherfield shrubbery and he invites her to join them she says pointedly; 'No, no stay where you are, you are charmingly grouped and appear to uncommon advantage. The picturesque would be spoilt by admitting the fourth. Goodbye'.

After further trials and tribulations with Mr Darcy, Elizabeth's projected Lakes tour with her relatives takes place. 'Adieu to disappointment and spleen', she cries; 'What are men to rocks and mountains? Oh! what hours of transport we shall spend!' Mr Gardiner's business appointments were, in the event, to curtail Elizabeth's tour to the Lakes to permit only a visit to Derbyshire. 'Elizabeth was excessively disappointed, she had set her heart on seeing the Lakes', but soon cheerfully reconciled herself to visiting 'all the celebrated beauties of Matlock, Chatsworth, Dovedale, or the Peak'.

Jane Austen was also denied a Lakes tour, but in the summer of 1806, when staying five weeks with her cousins the Coopers at Hamstall Ridware, she would have had plenty of time to take Elizabeth's tour and proceed into Derbyshire. As Cassandra was of the party there would have been no letters from her sister to describe the tour, but it would probably have been the same as that recorded by Mrs Lybbe Powys, the diarist, who was Caroline Cooper's mother; from Hamstall Ridware to Cromford and along the via Gellia to Matlock and Dovedale.

The Austens' picturesque excursion would have been a rewarding experience, and writing to her sister in 1808 Jane Austen was rather superior about the Miss Ballards, who, in spite of being said to be 'remarkably well-informed', obviously did not live up to their own standards so that she could not 'discover any right they had by Taste or Feeling to go their late Tour'.

Jane Austen had, in any case, learnt from Gilpin's Tour all she needed to know about the district and the contrast of grey limestone rocks and rich tints of hanging woods that characterised the picturesque landscape her heroine Elizabeth Bennet visited. In terms of 'Taste and Feeling' she had found no difficulty in giving Mr Darcy's Derbyshire estate of Pemberley a correctly picturesque setting in *Pride and Prejudice*.

GILPIN'S ILLUSTRATION TO SHOW THAT THREE COWS AND NO MORE ARE THE IDEAL NUMBER IN A COMPOSITION. JANE AUSTEN WAS CLEARLY DELIGHTED BY THIS NOTION. 'NO NO STAY WHERE YOU ARE, YOU ARE CHARMINGLY GROUPED', SAYS ELIZABETH BENNET.

THE
BEAUTIFUL
GROUNDS
AT
PEMBERLEY

IN PAINTINGS SUCH AS THIS JOSEPH WRIGHT OF DERBY
SHOWED THE PICTURESQUE NATURE OF HIS HOME COUNTY.
MR DARCY'S PEMBERLEY WAS SITED IN DERBYSHIRE
AND ELIZABETH BENNET AND THE GARDINERS TOURED
MATLOCK AND DOVEDALE BEFORE THEY VISITED IT.
THE AUSTENS MAY HAVE MADE A SIMILAR TOUR IN 1806.

Pemberley and its beautiful grounds play an important part in the plot of *Pride and Prejudice*. The heroine, who had been so prejudiced against Mr Darcy on first impressions, had to be shown that he was a man of morals and of good taste. What better than to give him a landscape of which Gilpin, Jane Austen's 'best of men', would have approved; a landscape in character with his picturesque Derbyshire scene? The novelist's ruse was entirely satisfactory as Elizabeth was delighted by Pemberley; and when after several more eventful chapters she tells her sister that she has become engaged to Mr Darcy, and Jane asks incredulously when this extraordinary change of attitude had taken place, Elizabeth playfully replies; 'It has been coming on so gradually, that I hardly know when it began. But I believe I must date it from my first seeing his beautiful grounds at Pemberley'.

When Jane Austen wrote this at the end of the eighteenth century, a controversy was raging as to what might be termed 'beautiful' in country house landscapes. The 'formal mockery of princely gardens' with flights of terraces, cascades, fountains and parterres had long since largely been banished in England in favour of gardens modelled on nature; but this was beautiful nature, not wild nature. The aim of cultivating 'Beautiful Nature' in mid-eighteenth-century grounds was best described by the Palladian Isaac Ware in 1750; 'What we propose now in Gardens is to collect the beauties of Nature and to separate them from those rude views in which her blemishes are seen, to bring them nearer the eye, and to dispose them in the most pleasing order and create an universal harmony'.

Beautiful forms, such as Hogarth's serpentine line from his *Analysis of Beauty* (1753) or Burke's definition of beauty in his *Philosophical Enquiry into the Origin of our Ideas of the Sublime and the Beautiful* (1757), dominated ideas in Georgian decorative art and gardening. Smoothness, Burke said, was 'a quality so essential to beauty that I do not recollect anything beautiful that is not smooth;... smooth slopes of earth in gardens; smooth streams in the landscape, in fine women smooth skins and in several sorts of ornamental furniture, smooth and polished surfaces'. Smooth beauty in landscape produced an effect of satisfaction and agreeable relaxation.

Lancelot Brown, known as 'Capability' Brown, became the professional practitioner of such beautiful, satisfying landscape with smooth lawns and slopes, serpentine rivers, clumps of trees and open views. Horace Walpole thought that when Brown's Petworth Park gained 'venerable maturity' it would show everything that the eighteenth century set out to achieve in 'modern gardening'. Jane Austen would have seen many engravings of Brown landscapes in books of gentlemen's seats and probably knew Highclere, laid out by Brown in 1770, not far from Steventon.

Samuel Richardson's *Sir Charles Grandison*, from which Jane Austen dramatised scenes for family performance, gives a typical Brown layout to Grandison Hall

GILPIN'S *FOREST SCENERY*, HIS PICTURESQUE OBSERVATIONS ON THE NEW FOREST, INFLUENCED SENSITIVE IMPROVERS. GILPIN GREATLY ADMIRED DUTCH PAINTINGS OF WOODY LANDSCAPES SUCH AS THIS RUYSDAEL.

A 'FOREST LAWN' SCENE IN THE NEW FOREST WHICH GILPIN PREFERRED TO A LANDSCAPED LAWN.

and so reflects the hero's aristocratic standards at a time when morals and taste were linked. The 'gardens and lawns seen from the windows of the spacious house' were 'as boundless as the mind of the owner and as free and open as his countenance'. Grandison Hall had the essential Brown feature of a sunk fence or ha-ha so that 'the eye is carried to views that have no bounds'. Although Sir Charles was her paragon of virtue and Jane Austen's family recalled that 'all that was ever said or done in the cedar parlour' of Grandison Hall was remembered by her, Sir Charles's views on landscaping were forty years out of date; Mr Darcy needed a different style of landscape to show off his 'Taste and Feeling' and it was to Gilpin that Jane Austen turned for guidance on the layout of Pemberley.

For Elizabeth Bennet 'beautiful grounds' did not signify Burkean ideals of abstract beauty. Pemberley's attraction was Gilpin's picturesque beauty, where nature's 'rude views' were not rejected and the characteristic abruptness of the Derbyshire scene was preferred to smoothness and 'gradual deviations'. Elizabeth felt that 'she had never seen a place for which nature had done more'; this was not the gracefully elegant nature of 'Capability' Brown or Grandison Hall but the nature that William Gilpin had taught Jane Austen's generation to seek out and admire with a picturesque eye.

Although, in retrospect, Gilpin was seen to have been very influential on the later phase of landscape improvement, he had never intended to do more than awaken an interest in natural scenery through the amusement of picturesque travel. His friends and champions, William Mason and Horace Walpole, who had first encouraged him to write up his tours, persuaded him, in the fifteen years that elapsed before publication, to include comments on what he called 'artificial scenery'. His remarks were so valid in the context of his general comments on picturesque beauty that John Claudius Loudon in his widely-read *Encyclopaedia* of 1820 advised that 'the whole of his tours and writings on the Picturesque will merit the study of the landscape gardener'.

Gilpin had never considered the possibility of extending his picturesque ideas to improving landscape, as Uvedale Price was later to do in his *Essay on the Picturesque* in 1794 which bore the sub-title 'on the Use of Studying Pictures for the Purpose of Improving Real Landscape'. When Gilpin rearranged nature on picturesque principles, as Henry Tilney, after delivering his 'lecture on the picturesque', had done up Beechen Cliff, this was an imaginary exercise; he had not advocated actually manipulating scenery to make a park or garden worthy of painting. Payne Knight and Uvedale Price, who both lived in picture-worthy Herefordshire and undertook their own improvements, deplored professional landscaping undertaken to a formula, and were particularly critical of Brown's work.

Humphry Repton explained what happened after Brown's death in 1783; he 'was immediately succeeded by a numerous herd of his foremen and working

gardeners, who, from having executed his designs, became consulted, as well as employed, in the several works he had entrusted them to superintend'. Without the master's genius a great mansion came to stand incongruously in what Payne Knight ridiculed in his poem *The Landscape* in 1794 as 'shaven lawns, that far around it creep in one eternal undulating sweep'.

Gilpin largely ignored Price and Knight, but he had already made his own criticism of landscaped lawns after he went to live in the New Forest in 1778 and became enchanted with its 'forest lawns' grazed by cattle in the depth of the forest. 'What are the lawns of Hagley, or any other place celebrated for this species of artificial landscape, but paltry imitations of the genuine works of Nature?' he asked in his *Forest Scenery*, published in 1791, but written many years before. In the preface he stated that he had had little intention of,

> amusing myself any more with writing on picturesque subjects. But one scene drew me on to another; till at length I had traversed the whole forest. The subject was new to me. I had been much among lakes, and mountains: but I had never lived in a forest.

Gilpin had always admired the 'close forest scenery' depicted in Dutch paintings with their 'observance of the minutiae of nature'; and 'how the bold protuberances of an old trunk received the light, and shade – how easily the large boughs parted; and how negligently the smaller were interwoven – how elegantly the foliage hung; and what various shapes its little tuftings exhibited'.

In *Forest Scenery* Gilpin noted not only natural forest scenery but landscape improvements in the area, which would have interested the 'Hampshire-born' Austens. There was no question in his mind of censuring Brown's landscaping out of hand. He referred to Brown, in *Forest Scenery*, as 'an ingenious improver' and had nothing but praise for his capabilities at Cadland, 'the seat of Mr Drummond', overlooking the Solent.

> The clumps particularly he has managed with great judgement. We observed some combination of ash, and other trees, which were equal to any clumps we had ever seen. They adorned the natural scene, and were just such as the picturesque eye would introduce in artificial landscape.

Gilpin's first experience of the landscape style in gardening had been in 1748 when he visited Stowe, which he much admired. He was later so struck with Charles Hamilton's Painshill that he devoted a whole sketchbook to what he clearly saw as picturesque scenes. He appreciated that an owner surrounded by rugged, wild scenery would need to make some concessions to domesticity and conceded in his Lake Tour, published in 1786, that; 'The business of the embellished scene is to make

J.M.W. TURNER'S *HAREWOOD HOUSE FROM THE SOUTH*. TURNER PAINTED SEVERAL VIEWS OF THIS BEAUTIFUL LANDSCAPE OF 'SMOOTHNESS AND GRADUAL DEVIATION' AS IMPROVED BY COWPER'S 'OMNIPOTENT MAGICIAN', 'CAPABILITY' BROWN.

everything convenient and comfortable around the house – to remove offensive objects, and to add a pleasing foreground to the distance'.

Gilpin praises 'the embellished garden and the park scene' where;

in England alone the pure model of nature is adopted... as we seek among the wild works of nature for the sublime, we seek here for the beautiful; and where there is a variety of lawn, wood and water, and these naturally combined; and not too much decorated with buildings, nor disgraced by fantastic ornaments; we find a species of landscape, which no country but England can display in such perfection; not only because this just taste in decoration prevails nowhere else; but also because no where else are found such proper materials.

As G.W Johnson in his *History of Gardening* wrote of Gilpin in 1829; 'His writings are in a most agreeable style and were generally read. If it is too much to say that they formed the national taste, they served most effectually to correct it'. Through the analysis of scenery in his picturesque tours Gilpin had introduced the concept of 'the character of the region' for the benefit of the traveller; it soon became apparent that an improver should not apply a standard landscape formula anywhere in the country. Gilpin condemned, whoever had designed it, any intended improvement which was not in keeping with the character of the region; any ostentatious structure, planting, or artificial piece of water, out of place in natural scenery, he called, in no uncertain terms, 'awkward' or 'disgusting'.

One such criticism in *Forest Scenery* was levelled against Paultons, sited on the Cadnam in Gilpin's beloved New Forest. Although he reserved his judgement on Brown's planting there, Gilpin strongly objected to the damming up of the little forest stream and its transformation into an artificial piece of water and was particularly severe about the glaring white Chinese bridge built to adorn it. 'We wish for simple ornaments on all occasions – ornaments which the eye is not obliged to notice', he wrote. Mason pointed out to Gilpin that the Chinese bridge was almost certainly due to the owner's and not Brown's awkward taste, as was often the case.

No such lapse of judgement on the part of the owner would of course be allowed at Pemberley, where, in front of the house,

a stream of some natural importance was swelled into a greater, but without any artificial appearance. Its banks were neither formal, nor falsely adorned. Elizabeth was delighted. She had never seen a place for which nature had done more, or where natural beauty had been so little counteracted by an awkward taste.

Mr Darcy, as a bonus to his good taste, had been able to retain his trout stream, the use of which he so civilly offered to Mr Gardiner, whereas many landowners who

STOURHEAD'S CIRCUIT WALK LOOKED ON TO CONTRIVED PICTURESQUE VISTAS AND NOT ON TO NATURAL SCENERY.

THE TYPE OF BALD AND BARE LANDSCAPE REGARDED AS FALSE TASTE BY THE PICTURESQUE IMPROVERS.

had had pieces of water made regretted the loss of their free-flowing trout streams. The only bridge that crossed the stream was a simple one of which Gilpin would have approved, 'in character with the general air of the scene'.

At Pemberley the surrounding Derbyshire beauties were not exhibited merely as the 'stare view' many of Brown's wealthy clients demanded from the principal windows of the house; the 'boundless' prospect that delighted Sir Charles Grandison from Grandison Hall. Elizabeth Bennet noted with approval, as the housekeeper took them round, that the river, the high woody hills and the winding valley were seen in different aspects from every room, in such a way that 'from every window there were beauties to be seen'. The house was also picturesquely situated on 'rising ground and backed by a ridge of high woody hills' and not presented, four-square in the landscape, as a 'stare view' to the neighbourhood; only after the visitor had entered the lodge and had driven for some time through Pemberley Woods was it seen from 'the top of a considerable eminence, where the wood ceased, and the eye was instantly caught by Pemberley House, situated on the opposite side of a valley, into which the road with some abruptness wound'.

Mr Darcy's Pemberley had a notable circuit walk through its 'beautiful grounds', which was the landscape gardening counterpart of a Gilpin picturesque tour, exploited by his friend William Mason. Gilpin had never advocated contriving picturesque features within the garden, particularly Salvator Rosa like effects; what was required was for a landlord with naturally picturesque scenery to display it to advantage. Gilpin's patron and former pupil at Cheam, William Mitford, who had presented him to the Boldre living in the New Forest, had a fine circuit walk at Exbury overlooking the Beaulieu river and Isle of Wight, which Gilpin praises in *Forest Scenery* as showing how the 'natural advantages of the scene' can be judiciously exploited 'in good hands'. By 1791 Mitford would undoubtedly have taken advantage of the advice of his friends Gilpin and Mason.

William Lock of Norbury, another friend and patron of Gilpin, also had a circuit walk, which Jane Austen would have known as it bordered Great Bookham where she often stayed with her relatives, the Cookes. In his Western Tour in 1798 Gilpin described how along the walk the panoramic views over the Surrey Hills, including the 'celebrated Box Hill', were made into peephole scenes through framed planting and shown to picturesque advantage.

The early landscaped gardens such as Stowe, Studley Royal and Stourhead had walks with designed vistas, but these were orientated on man-made internal scenery and buildings, especially temples, whereas picturesque circuit walks looked beyond the garden into natural scenery and the prospect was broken down into a series of framed peephole scenes, where the viewing points corresponded to the 'stations'

THE CHINESE BRIDGE AT PAULTONS.
GILPIN CONDEMNED ANY OSTENTATIOUS
STRUCTURE OR ARTIFICAL PIECE OF WATER
AS OUT OF PLACE IN NATURAL SCENERY.
JANE AUSTEN TOOK GOOD CARE THAT
MR DARCY'S PEMBERLEY HAD NO
SUCH 'AWKWARD TASTE'.

Gilpin recommended to picturesque tourists. The varied arrangement of the walks and the foreground planting along them was crucial to the success of 'hide and discover' views for which William Mason gave detailed instruction in his poem *The English Garden*.

> *How long so'ever the wanderer roves, each step*
> *Shall wake fresh beauties: each short point present*
> *A different picture, new, and yet the same.*

Mason was unsuccessful in persuading Gilpin to write a prose version of his poetical gardening treatise, but this was undertaken by William Burgh, whose comments on the above lines read;

> A path is a series of foregrounds; and to adapt each part of this to the various combinations of the distant objects, which always result from the change of place or aspect, is the proper business of art... such interruptions as may frequently give the charm of renewal to what we had for a time been deprived of.

Jane Austen describes, in unusual detail, such a picturesque circuit walk at Pemberley, which varied the scene with hide and discover views and Gilpinesque stations.

> They entered the woods, and bidding adieu to the river for a while, ascended some of the higher grounds; whence, in spots where the opening of the trees gave the eye power to wander, were many charming views of the valley, the opposite hills, with the long range of woods overspreading many, and occasionally part of the stream.... they pursued the accustomed circuit; which brought them again, after some time, in a descent among hanging woods, to the edge of the water, in one of its narrowest parts. They crossed it by a simple bridge, in character with the general air of the scene; it was a spot less adorned than any they had yet visited; and the valley, here contracted into a glen, allowed room only for the stream, and a narrow walk amidst the rough coppice-wood, which bordered it.

THE ILAM CIRCUIT WALK ALONG THE MANIFOLD IS REMINISCENT OF JANE AUSTEN'S DESCRIPTION OF THE PEMBERLEY WALKS.

The glen had been left in its rough state without clearings, as Gilpin had advocated in his description of glen scenery in *Forest Scenery*. He told landlords lucky enough to have a glen in their grounds to avoid any thoughts of improvement.

You cannot well have a more fortunate circumstance. But great care should be taken not to load it with ornament. Such scenes admit little art. Their beauty consists in their natural wildness.

Areas cleared for seats or conspicuous openings in glens were 'awkward, and disgusting'.

Pemberley is a fictitious literary landscape created in the same way that Gilpin said he composed his picturesque landscapes; ideas are taken from the general face of the country, not from any particular scene. Jane Austen obviously gave a great deal of thought to Pemberley and has a clear plan of the house in her mind. On Elizabeth Bennet's second visit to Pemberley as an invited guest, she goes through the hall to the saloon which looked out on to the 'high woody hills' that had been described as backing the house, two chapters before, when she approached the front of the house as a tourist. Cassandra may even have drawn a sketch of the imagined Pemberley landscape with its 'great variety of ground' to fix it in her sister's mind for her.

Chatsworth has been suggested for Pemberley, because Jane Austen teasingly placed it in the vicinity of Bakewell, but Darcy was no Duke of Devonshire and Chatsworth could not be kept up on even £10,000 a year. Significantly Gilpin was unimpressed by Chatsworth, which he considered retained many of the old artificial formalities. He did, however, describe one mansion, in the Dovedale section of his Lakes Tour, which would have been of use and interest to Jane Austen's picturesque deliberations. Ilam was described by Gilpin as, 'a very characteristic scene', with the house standing on a hill, 'which slopes gently in front but is abrupt and broken behind'. He noted the 'bold, woody bank' where 'pleasing walks might be formed'; a circuit walk was later made above the Manifold, a trout stream enjoyed by Isaac Walton. Very little had been done at Ilam 'to embellish its natural situation', but in the immediate surroundings Gilpin condemned a formal flower garden by the house which he thought was at total variance with the scene. Mr Darcy did not err in this way at Pemberley; only 'beautiful oaks and Spanish chestnuts' were 'scattered over the intermediate lawn' between the house and the stream.

Jane Austen would have seen Ilam, also much admired by Dr Johnson, if she made a Dovedale tour from Hamstall Ridware in 1806, but by then the Pemberley chapters had almost certainly been written, based on her concentrated reading of Gilpin. *First Impressions*, the first version of *Pride and Prejudice*, was said by Cassandra to have been begun in 1796, possibly while she was staying, in the autumn, with her brother Edward, who had had the benefit of a northern tour; the date is confirmed by Elizabeth Bennet's answer to Lady Catherine de Bourgh, who demanded to know how old she was; 'I am not yet one and twenty', she replied coyly. The author's twenty-first birthday would have been only a few months away.

We know that the future *Pride and Prejudice* was for Jane Austen 'my own darling child' and Elizabeth Bennet as 'delightful a creature as every appeared in print'; the novel was also a family favourite and it would have seemed incredible to them that it was rejected by the publisher in 1797. They continued to read it aloud and bring the characters to life even after it was finally published in 1813. When Jane Austen visited a London exhibition that year she spent some time looking for portraits which would do justice to her newly-wed Jane and Elizabeth Bennet and told her sister in a letter that she had been delighted to find Mrs Bingley 'dressed in a white gown, with green ornaments, which convinces me of what I had always supposed, that green was a favourite colour with her'. She did not find a satisfying Mrs Darcy.

However much *Pride and Prejudice* was 'lop't and crop't' in the 1812 revision to reduce it from its original three long volumes, the main plot and scenes would have been in place; its youthful 'bright and sparkling' playful quality shines through even after the editing by the more mature novelist. If the Austens did travel picturesquely into Derbyshire in 1806, and, by way of souvenirs, rob Mr Darcy's county of a 'few petrified spars' of the kind Gilpin had described in his Tour, they would surely have had much amusement in trying to find a spot which would do justice to the Gilpin-inspired 'beautiful grounds at Pemberley'.

A MERE NOTHING BEFORE REPTON

REPTON'S RED BOOK FOR STONELEIGH ABBEY IS
IMMORTALISED IN *MANSFIELD PARK*.

The first of the novels which belong to the Chawton period of Jane Austen's career was *Mansfield Park*. She began it in 1811 whilst still revising *Pride and Prejudice*. The subdued Cowper-addicted heroine, Fanny Price, is the antithesis of the sparkling Elizabeth Bennet and there is a moral seriousness in the new novel which contrasts with the playful tone of *Pride and Prejudice*. Two whole chapters of *Mansfield Park* are devoted to improvement; actual techniques of landscape gardening and the moral issues involved. Mr Darcy's 'beautiful grounds at Pemberley' are a credit to the landlord's own impeccable 'Taste and Feeling', while Sotherton, Mr Rushworth's country house in Mansfield Park, is highlighted as a place where the owner had to avail himself of the services of a professional landscape gardener. While Pemberley's literary landscape was an imaginary Gilpinesque scene, that at Sotherton relates to a real situation that Jane Austen knew well – Repton's improvements at her cousin's Stoneleigh Abbey in Warwickshire.

Humphry Repton took centre stage in the Regency period and published four influential books on landscape gardening as well as one on his designs for the Royal Pavilion at Brighton. Although he worked on the established principles of eighteenth-century landscape gardening, he reintroduced 'dressed grounds' near the house for the owner's comfort and so also catered for the revived interest in horticulture. Repton was the first practitioner to adopt the title landscape gardener, which figures prominently on his trade card. 'Capability' Brown was usually referred to as a 'place-maker'. Gilpin, who died in 1804, knew very little about Repton and never used the term landscape gardener in his writings; nor did Jane Austen, although she had every opportunity to do so when she discussed Repton's work in *Mansfield Park* and even calmly stated his fees.

Repton admired Gilpin, whose works he studied as part of his 'breviary'. He was an excellent watercolourist, very much in the Gilpin style. Hitherto professionals had usually produced plans of layouts for their clients but Repton presented them with attractive watercolour drawings of what their grounds would look like after his services, usually in the form of volumes bound in red and known as Red Books. The watercolours showing the unimproved scene he found on arrival had a hinged overlay, which when lifted revealed a delightful Repton transformation; the accompanying text recalled 'conversations on-the-spot' with the client, whose good taste, if only in calling him in, is applauded. There are many amusing touches in the painted scenes; one which would have delighted Jane Austen, if she could have seen the manuscript, was a before and after picturesque grouping of three cows *à la* Gilpin, with two cows in the unimproved watercolour and a third just peeping out from under the flap. However, their cousin's impressive Red Book for Stoneleigh Abbey provided her with all she needed for a skit on Repton's landscape gardening in *Mansfield Park*.

REPTON'S TRADE CARD.
JANE AUSTEN JUDGED PROFESSIONAL
LANDSCAPE IMPROVEMENTS BY
MORAL, RATHER THAN AESTHETIC
STANDARDS.

Jane Austen's first real acquaintance with Repton's work was at Adlestrop in Gloucestershire, where her cousin the Revd Thomas Leigh had consulted him in 1799. When she visited Adlestrop with her mother and sister in 1806 Repton's work had been completed at a cost of '5 gns a day' and reference made to it in his *Observations on the Theory and Practice of Landscape Gardening*, published in 1803. According to his account book, the Revd Thomas only paid two guineas for the book, which may have been a concession to clients as the advertised price was four guineas. *Observations*, which Jane Austen had the opportunity of seeing in her cousin's library, contained Repton's mature deliberations on his art and quoted many extracts from Red Books, showing his overlay technique.

One of the overlays which seems to have engaged her attention was that for Sufton Court in Herefordshire, which showed the effect of breaking up a formal row of trees in front of the drawing room to improve the prospect. 'In some situations', Repton said, 'improvement may be effected by the axe rather than by the spade, of which this sketch furnishes an instance'. Jane Austen would already have seen the axe at work at Herriards House, near Steventon, where Repton's improvements had involved destroying half an avenue of silver firs; also the extent of tree-axing clearance needed at Blaise Castle to achieve its admired romantic prospects. Mr Rushworth in *Mansfield Park*, who had been so impressed by Repton's improvements at his friend's place at 'Compton', had, although slow in the uptake, taken the point;

There had been two or three fine old trees cut down that grew too near the house, and it opens up the prospect amazingly, which makes me think that Repton, or any body of that sort, would certainly have the avenue at Sotherton down.

In the advertisement at the beginning of *Observations*, Repton explains the nature of his work in attempting to establish fixed principles in landscape gardening, based on his considerable experience in the field. In reference to his Red Books Repton says, 'thus my opinions have been diffused over the kingdom in nearly two hundred such manuscript volumes'. Although, unfortunately, there appears to have been no such presentation for Adlestrop, Jane Austen would already have detected from his published comments what Mason called 'a little of the coxcomb' in Repton. She would also have been amused by his accompanying trade card, wittily appropriating Milton:

> *Straight mine eye hath caught new pleasures*
> *While the landskip round it measures.*

Repton stated in *Observations* that improvements at Adlestrop had been made 'in full view both of the mansion and the parsonage', which made it an unusual assignment. The Revd Thomas had superintended and settled Repton's account for the improvements of the whole Adlestrop estate, owned by his nephew James Henry

REPTON RE-ROUTED THE ACCESS TO ADLESTROP HOUSE WHICH SHOWED THE SANDERSON MILLER FAÇADE TO ADVANTAGE.

A BATH HOUSE DESIGNED FOR MRS JAMES HENRY LEIGH BY REPTON'S ARCHITECT SON,
JOHN ADEY, BY THE STREAM AT ADLESTROP.

Leigh at the big house. James Henry was only a child when his father died and left his brother the Revd Thomas to manage the estate. Thomas Leigh was by nature an improver; he had already, while his brother was alive, enclosed the village green by agreement and exchange of glebeland and planted out the cottages in order to extend the rectory garden.

His wife, Mary, who was also a Leigh and his first cousin, was not in favour of improvement, and significantly it was not until after her death in 1797 that Repton was invited to Adlestrop to merge the garden of the rectory with his nephew's 100 acres to give the effect of a gentleman's residence in a park. To achieve this the entrance of the rectory was moved and a road diverted in 1803; some of the front doors of the roadside cottages can now, after the Revd Thomas's improvements, be seen at the back of their houses. The Repton rectory garden at what was now the back of his house sloped down to a new artificial lake.

When Mrs Austen arrived at her cousin's new establishment her reaction must have been the same as Mr Rushworth's in *Mansfield Park* when he saw what 'Smith' had done for 'Compton' 'I never saw a place so altered in my life. I told Smith I did not know where I was'. The whole idea must have intrigued Jane Austen and we can only suppose that she had her cousin's rectory improvements in mind when, in *Mansfield Park*, Henry Crawford, the Reptonian improver, in the middle of a game of cards, gives Edmund Bertram instructions on how to improve his rectory at Thornton Lacey in a similar fashion.

Edmund is advised to turn the house in a different direction, making a new entrance through the present garden and making a new garden at what is now the back of the house, taking in the meadows and doing something with the stream so that by 'judicious improvement' the parsonage house could be turned into a 'residence of a man of education, taste, modern manners and good connections'; the last sentence exactly resembles the sort of flattery Repton always handed out in correspondence to a prospective client and Henry Crawford, who it is claimed could 'see quickly' and 'resolve quickly and act quickly', appears to have the requisite 'knowledge of effects before they are produced' that Repton, in his *Observations*, asserts a 'professor' of landscape gardening should possess.

A new approach road was made through the park connecting Adlestrop House and rectory, which showed the beautiful new Sanderson Miller façade of the 1760s to great advantage. 'The approach now is one of the finest things in the country. You see the house in a most surprising manner', Mr Rushworth had said of Repton's new approach to his friend Smith's 'Compton'. It was one of Repton's tenets that the approach should not be considered as a parade to the house, neither formally through a straight avenue, nor unnecessarily circuitously to show off extent of

property; it should be 'presented in a pleasing point of view' at an advantageous stage in the approach and then as soon as visible 'there should be no temptation to quit it'.

Although there are no before and after Repton scenes for Adlestrop, Jane Austen had the advantage of knowing what the garden at the mansion house had looked like before improvement, as it was written up by Mary Leigh in her *History of the Leigh family of Adlestrop* in 1788 for the benefit of James Henry Leigh for whom she and the Revd Thomas had acted as guardians. She wrote of its pleasures in his grandfather's day with a canal, fountains and alcoves and then the later 'modernising' in a naturalistic style by his father in the mid-1760s to accompany the Sanderson Miller garden front, with the canal made sinuous, rococo buildings and a pool near the house. Repton was later to remove this pool in his landscaping as he said, in his *Observations*, that 'it lessened the place, by attracting the eye and preventing its range over the lawn and falling ground beyond'; instead to the side of the house he diverted a little stream of water, and later his son designed a delightful canvas bath house, whose footings beside it can still be seen.

Jane Austen, like her mother's cousin Mary, was extremely interested in the Leigh family, their origins and royalist connections. Their founding father was the Elizabethan Sir Thomas Leigh, who had been Lord Mayor of London and rode before the queen to her proclamation; a real Dick Whittington, who had come down from Cheshire to be apprenticed to Sir Rowland Hill, an influential City man who took a fancy to him. He acquired property at Stoneleigh and Adlestrop and it was his eldest son Rowland, named after their benefactor, whose niece and heiress he married, who inherited and enlarged both estates. At his death in 1571 the estates were divided, the bulk in Gloucestershire going to the eldest and the Warwickshire property to the second son.

It was from the senior line that Thomas and Mary Leigh and Jane Austen's mother, born Cassandra Leigh, were descended; their respective fathers had been born at Adlestrop and the eldest, William, Thomas's father, inherited; when he died in 1757, James, the eldest son, followed and Thomas took the Adlestrop living, having married his cousin, Mary Leigh. After Mary died, his sister Elizabeth, a great favourite of the Austen family and Cassandra's godmother, went to look after him at the rectory.

All the Leighs were strong royalist supporters, including Jane Austen, who wrote of the Stuarts in her Goldsmith's *A History of England* that they were 'a family who were always ill-used, Betrayed and Neglected, whose virtues are seldom allowed, while their errors are never forgotten'. Mary Leigh told in her history, written to inspire James Henry, the new inheritor of Adlestrop, how his home had been known as 'a staunch asylum to every friend of the royalist cause' and how

OVERLEAF: REPTON'S BEFORE ILLUSTRATION OF THE SOUTH FRONT AT STONELEIGH BEING STAKED OUT TO BRING THE AVON NEARER THE HOUSE. THE RESULT, WITH WATTEAUESQUE 'RICH EMBELLISHMENTS', APPEARS ON PAGE 91.

Theophilus, who was also of great interest to Jane Austen as he was her mother's grandfather, turned out the men of Adlestrop to oppose the landing of William III, but got no further than Cirencester.

As a protest to the Hanoverians, however, Theophilus continued to carry 'the manners of his youth to his old age', as did his son William, Mary and Cassandra Leigh's uncle. Mary paints a picture of him as a Roger de Coverley Tory squire and regrets that the bowling green was removed in the 1760 garden improvement, which she herself remembered as 'one of the best accustomed greens in England; for there was seldom a fine day in which your hospitable grandfather surrounded by his neighbours did not use it'.

Shortly before the Austens went to stay at Adlestrop in 1806 the news came through that, owing to an unexpected will, the Revd Thomas had inherited Stoneleigh, the property of the ennobled, although cadet branch of the Leighs, thus uniting the Leigh properties in one family after two centuries. The Revd Thomas invited his cousins to accompany him on an immediate expedition of reconnaissance from Adlestrop. Jane Austen set off with great excitement to see what she later described as 'one of the finest estates in England', which was of even greater interest as a stronghold of the 'loyal Leighs' and their royalist sympathies than Adlestrop. Charles I had sheltered at Stoneleigh with 600 horsemen after the gates of Coventry were shut against him, for which Thomas Leigh was created Baron Leigh at Oxford in 1643, when it was the royalist capital; and, in 1745, their loyalty to the Stuart cause undiminished, the Leighs prepared to receive the Young Pretender at Stoneleigh.

As Jacobites the Leighs kept away from Court and public affairs and lived in retirement surrounded by their family portraits and those of the discredited Stuarts; their furniture was carved and emblazoned with the Leigh arms in a pre-Hanoverian style. Jane Austen's first encounter with her ancestors' Stoneleigh Abbey is one of the strongest autobiographical episodes relived in her writing as the guided tour of the Rushworths' newly-inherited Sotherton in *Mansfield Park*, with its old-fashioned elegance of 'shining floors, solid mahogany, rich damask, marble, gilding and carving'. We share Jane Austen's delight as Fanny Price shows a keen interest in the portraits and in 'all that Mrs Rushworth could relate of the family in former times, its rise and grandeur, regal visits and loyal efforts, delighted to connect anything with history already known, or warm her imagination with scenes of the past'.

The Leighs' loyalty extended to worshipping in their own chapel in order to avoid joining in prayers for the house of Hanover at their parish church. Fanny's romantic sense of history, stimulated by Scott's description of the loyal past enshrined in the gothic chapel of 'fair Melrose', received a rude shock when the party entered the Sotherton chapel. At Stoneleigh, as at Sotherton, Jane Austen found that the

chapel is one of many rooms on the ground floor and has a gallery which was entered from the family apartments above. The crimson velvet cushions still appear over the mahogany ledge of the gallery just as Fanny saw them at Sotherton.

Fanny's reaction to the chapel-room, where 'no Scottish monarch sleeps below', must surely reflect Jane Austen's own disappointment and, like Fanny, she had to be reminded that she must go to the parish church to see the family's 'banners and atchievements'. The Revd Thomas discontinued the practice of using the private chapel and thereafter, when at Stoneleigh, worshipped with his parishioners; he continued to fulfil his own clerical duties at Adlestrop.

We are fortunate in having a letter from Mrs Austen to her daughter-in-law which tells of their astonishment at the size and grandeur of Stoneleigh Abbey. Their thoughts must have been very much on Catherine Morland as she approached Northanger Abbey full of gothic expectations and Mrs Austen remarks on 'the state bedchamber with a dark crimson Velvet Bed: an alarming apartment just fit for a heroine'. Like Northanger Abbey only a few of the old rooms remained and the only real part of the original abbey was the cloisters and the vaulted cellars and kitchens. 'The house is larger than I could have supposed', she said. 'We can now find our way about it, I mean the best part; as to the offices (which were the old abbey) Mr Leigh almost despairs of ever finding his way about them. I have proposed his setting up Direction Posts at the angles'.

Jane Austen's revelations on the Stoneleigh landscape improvements, in the guise of Sotherton, derive from two separate experiences; her cousin's thoughts on their first sight of the old-fashioned grounds and the reading of Repton's proposals in his Red Book some years later when the situations at Compton and Sotherton could be brought into sharper focus: 'As he has done so well by Smith, I think I had better have him at once. His terms are 5 guineas a day', said Mr Rushworth contemplating his unimproved Sotherton; 'Smith's place is the admiration of all the country and it was a mere nothing before Repton took it in hand. I think I shall have Repton'.

Although Jane Austen had no intention of suggesting that the dim-witted Mr Rushworth resembled her 'respectable, worthy, clever, agreeable Mr Thomas Leigh', there is no doubt that these were his sentiments as he thought of Repton's handling of his own modest 100 acres at Adlestrop and considered what he might do for the 700 acre Stoneleigh estate by the Avon which he had just inherited;

> Smith has not much above 100 acres altogether in his grounds, which is little enough, and it makes it more surprising that the place can have been so improved. Now, at Sotherton, we have a good 700, without reckoning the water meadows; so that I think if so much could be done at Compton, we need not despair.

RIGHT: Repton called the Stoneleigh gatehouse 'an object of pleasure to those who delight in whatever is ancient and venerable and therefore worthy to be retained in modern days of upstart innovation'. A sentiment which Jane Austen would surely have echoed.

Repton was called in at Stoneleigh two years later and struck the usual obsequious note at the beginning of the Red Book presented to Thomas Leigh in 1809.

I am addressing myself to you, who have displayed so much good taste in what has been done at Adlestrop under your immediate direction and who have been pleased occasionally to consult me on that subject. – I must therefore congratulate you on having the more ample field to display your taste – at the same time that I congratulate the County on this most unusual domain (so long preserved in the same family) having now a possessor who knows both how to value and how to improve its natural beauties.

James Austen, who held the Cubbington living on the Stoneleigh estate but seldom visited, stayed at Stoneleigh with his family in the summer of 1809 just after the Red Book had appeared on the scene. Doubtless he was able to tell his sister, who like Fanny Price was anxious to hear about 'the progress of it all', what a splendid presentation Repton had made with particularly delightful watercolours.

The Leigh grounds at Stoneleigh were deliberately as old-fashioned as their cedar parlours and furniture to avoid any suggestion that improvements might imply Whig intentions; not surprisingly, Repton told his client in the same introduction that it presented 'circumstances very different from any other place in which I have ever been consulted'. There could have been no other noble mansion in the country which still had an enclosed bowling green near the house in 1806. Mary Leigh, who had regretted the removal of the Adlestrop bowling green would undoubtedly have approved of its loyal manifestation.

A PEEPHOLE VIEW SHOWING THE INTENDED BRIDGE,
THE CASCADE AND THE HOUSE AS SEEN FRON THE KNOLL
ABOVE THE HOUSE.

Stoneleigh had a walled entrance forecourt on the imposing west front, which had been added by Smith of Warwick in 1726. A walled enclosure was the first object for 'fault-finding' when Jane Austen's improver, Henry Crawford, led the party out to 'examine the capabilities of that end of the house'. Anticipating Repton he exclaimed, 'I see walls of great promise'. Repton's before and after illustrations show how essential the removal of these walls were. Jane Austen must have lifted the flap in his Red Book with great amusement to reveal the river, water meadows and the grove beyond the walls.

The Mansfield Park party had noted that there was a 'stream which might be made a great deal of'. Repton's major proposal was, in fact, to widen and alter the

course of the Avon and bring it nearer to the south front of the house; the mill race was to be made into an ornamental cascade. His beautiful twilight view of the conflux of the race and the river (page 78) Repton thought could have been 'if more finished a Ruysdael'. He suggested that a distant framed view of the house and this scene might be achieved by clearing a spot in the grove on rising ground, which he marked on a plan and referred to in Gilpinesque terms as a 'station'. His suggestion was carried out and the 'station' has ever since been known simply as The View.

'I SEE WALLS OF GREAT PROMISE': THE REMOVAL OF THE WALLS REVEALED THE WIDENED AVON, WATER MEADOWS AND GROVE BEYOND THE IMPRESSIVE WEST FRONT.

Henry Crawford, it will be re-membered, invited a party to follow him to just such a 'knoll not a half a mile off, which would give him the requisite command of the house'; this was after Fanny, who inevitably had grown tired of walking in the wilderness, had been left sitting on a seat looking over to this knoll, and was found by Henry Crawford, Miss Bertram and Mr Rushworth who re-sumed the improvement discussions with her. Mr Rushworth 'scarcely risked an original thought of his own beyond a wish that they had seen his friend Smith's place'. Rushworth had

chosen a good spot to recall his friend's 'Compton' alias Adlestrop as Repton had pointed out that he had already achieved there something similar to the framed view he proposed for Stoneleigh and humbly suggested in his Red Book that he had 'only to recommend the same good taste and management which has succeeded so well at Adlestrop, to produce still greater effects at Stoneleigh Abbey'.

The Austens' visit to Stoneleigh took place in the summer when they, like Miss Crawford, found it 'insufferably hot', and preferred walking in the woods, which Mrs Austen said were 'impenetrable to the sun even in the middle of an August day'. She wrote; 'I had figured to myself long Avenues dark Rookeries and Dismal Yew Trees, but there are no such melancholy things'. She clearly thought on the lines of her cousin Mary Leigh where improvement was concerned and saw little wrong with the gardens about which her cousin was so exercised. The scene that met the Austens at Stoneleigh was just as described at Sotherton.

Mrs Austen's particular delight was the kitchen garden in which 'quantities of small fruits exceed anything you can form an idea of'. She told her daughter-in-law that she did 'not fail to spend some time every day' there; which was all very reminiscent of Mrs Norris, one of Mrs Austen's favourite characters, and perhaps she too was guilty of 'spunging' a heath from the gardener to take back in the carriage, to the annoyance of her companions. Much to the Austens' amusement, Lady Saye and

Sele, the mother-in-law of James Henry Leigh, who was next in the line of succession, was also on reconnaissance at the time of the Stoneleigh takeover. The elderly Revd Thomas did in fact die in 1813 and it was just as well that Mr and Mrs James Henry Leigh had been party to the Repton landscaping proposals as they would be called upon to implement them.

We can only speculate as to what Jane Austen's own thoughts on the proposed Stoneleigh improvements were, but it must be remembered that it was Maria Bertram, whose judgement on other matters was shown to be so faulty, who advised the heir of an unimproved estate; 'Your best friend upon such an occasion would be Mr Repton, I imagine'; and it was the worldly Mary Crawford who said; 'Had I a place of my own in the country, I should be thankful to any Mr Repton, who would undertake it and give me as much beauty as he could for my money'.

CHAPTER EIGHT

THE
RESPONSIBLE
LANDLORD

———

THE LANDLORD OR HIS STEWARD OUT ON HIS ROUNDS.
JANE AUSTEN WROTE AT A TIME OF NATIONAL
CRISIS WHEN RESPONSIBLE LANDLORDS WERE MAKING
EFFORTS TO INCREASE WARTIME
FOOD PRODUCTION.

W e are left in no doubt whatsoever as to Jane Austen's opinion of the buildings and gardens of Donwell Abbey, the home of Mr Knightley, set in a Surrey landscape near Box Hill; it was 'just what it ought to be and looked what it was', she said pointedly in her new novel *Emma*, which she began to write early in 1814 while *Mansfield Park* was still at the publishers. 'Emma felt an increasing respect for it, as a residence of a family of such true gentility, untainted in blood and understanding' and the reader knows that, as with Elizabeth Bennet and Pemberley, it is only a matter of time before the heroine and the beautiful grounds will be united.

Mr Knightley of Donwell Abbey was in all respects a paragon of virtue and a responsible landlord and it seems that Reptonian improvement had never crossed his mind; he had even left the old fishponds of the abbey in place and enjoyed to the full 'its suitable, becoming, characteristic situation, low and sheltered – its ample gardens stretching down to meadows washed by a stream, of which the Abbey, with all the old neglect of prospect, had scarcely a sight'. Repton had consoled the Revd Thomas Leigh in his Red Book for Stoneleigh Abbey for this selfsame deficiency, that when the mansion was built after the Dissolution on the site of the old abbey 'little attention seems to have been given either to the Prospect or the Aspect' and that none of the main rooms took advantage of the river.

Jane Austen's mother confirmed that they generally sat in the small breakfast room at Stoneleigh Abbey because in all the vast array of rooms it was the only one, except the chapel, which had a view of the river; the rest of the south front was taken up by corridors and offices. Whereas Mr Knightley had made no attempt to rearrange his rambling old house to ameliorate its 'characteristic situation', Repton had proposed a new arrangement of rooms on the riverside front of Stoneleigh Abbey complete with external gallery. This was never built but Repton's proposal is the illustration on page 91 and on the jacket of this book.

In walking round the grounds of Donwell Abbey much is made of the very English 'sweet view – sweet to the eye and the mind' presented by the Abbey Mill Farm 'with meadows in front, and the river making a close and handsome curve round it', set in its 'rich pastures, spreading flocks, orchard in bloom and light col-umn of smoke ascending'. The smoke ascending from the abbey mill farm was a nice back-handed compliment to Repton, who in the Stoneleigh Red Book had illustrated the picturesque nature of smoke from rural buildings in the landscape. He professed to like cheerful scenes and decried the habit of removing habitation from landscaped parks, but in the case of the Stoneleigh Abbey mill was able to use its mill stream to great advantage in his picturesque river improvements.

The grounds of Donwell Abbey had an 'abundance of timber in rows and

avenues, which neither fashion nor extravagance had rooted up'. Fanny Price, who, in this matter, reflected Jane Austen's opinions, would have been delighted by them. She had been alarmed when possible improvements for Sotherton had first been discussed in *Mansfield Park* and heard that Repton would almost certainly cut down the avenue which was seen from the west windows of the house. 'Cut down an avenue. What a pity! Does it not make you think of Cowper? "Ye fallen avenues, once more I mourn your fate unmerited".' Fanny was unnecessarily concerned as in the Stoneleigh Red Book Repton only proposed to cut down two or three large trees which obstructed the western view of the river.

The possible loss of the avenue was viewed not so much on aesthetic grounds, but as a deliberate felling of what their favourite Cowper called 'patrimonial timber' and the consequent severing of its long association with the house. Elinor in *Sense and Sensibility* had been anxious to shield Marianne, who already had enough grief to bear, from the knowledge that their brother planned to remove the old walnuts on the knoll behind their former home at Norland to make way for his wife's new greenhouse and Reptonian flower garden.

Cowper called for a return to traditional, responsible attitudes to the land as when England was 'plain, hospitable, kind and undebauch'd'. He commended 'the venerable pile, th' abode of our forefathers – a grave whisker'd race, But tasteless' and condemned the frenzy of costly improvement, 'the idol of the age', where 'estates are landscapes' in the landowners' covetous eyes.

> *Mansions once*
> *Knew their own masters; and laborious hinds*
> *Who had surviv'd the father, serv'd the son.*

Mr Knightley's merit as a landlord went far beyond retaining his avenues and Jane Austen shows throughout *Emma* how the best interests of his estate and his tenants' welfare were put before any other consideration. He kept 'in hand the home farm at Donwell' and with the assistance of his trusted steward, William Larkins, kept himself informed about the state of the harvest, drainage, fencing, new seed drills, and cattle shows. Emma is interested in a discussion between Mr Knightley and his brother about the introduction·of a Scottish bailiff to a friend's estate, which suggests that he, and brother Edward, have possibly been studying J.C.Loudon's recently published *Observations on laying out Farms in the Scotch Style adapted to England*, based on his experimental farm at Great Tew, near Adlestrop. The Scottish system of crop rotation promised a better yield which would decrease the need for imported grain during the Napoleonic wars.

A great deal of productive land was taken up with growing oats for horses and responsible landlords were cutting down their equipage. We learn that Mr Knightley's horses were for use and seldom called upon to draw carriages. He was a magistrate and in touch with his parson and churchwarden about parish affairs and sent Donwell produce to needy parishioners. So important a part did William Larkins play in the affairs of Donwell that when Mr Knightley's love is finally declared and the question of living at Hartfield is raised, Emma playfully warns him, 'I am sure William Larkins will not like it. You must get his consent before you ask mine'. Cowper could not have asked for more!

The middle-aged Mr Knightley, as the responsible hero of *Emma*, was Edward Austen's favourite character and there was much of Edward to be seen in him; especially after he finally inherited the Knight estates, including Chawton, in 1812, in his early forties, and changed his name to Knight. When Jane Austen said that she 'must learn to make a better K', when writing to her brother, she had not yet conjured up the fictitious Mr Knightley in her imagination.

In *Mansfield Park*, which she was then writing, however, there is much of Edward in the sensible attitudes of the younger Edmund Bertram, especially towards improvement, which she had already witnessed at Godmersham. Mr Knightley and Edmund Bertram were linked together in the *Memoir* by James Edward Austen-Leigh when he wrote; 'She did not, however, suppose her imaginary characters were of a higher order than to be found in nature, for she said, when speaking of two of her

THE STREAM AT GODMERSHAM. EDWARD, LIKE MR DARCY AT PEMBERLEY,
RETAINED HIS TROUT STREAM AND HAD NOT MADE IT INTO AN ARTIFICIAL PIECE OF WATER.

great favourites, Edmund Bertram and Mr Knightley, "they are very far from being what I know English gentlemen often are".'

It was through Edward's good fortune in being adopted by the wealthy land-owning Knights that his sister came to know about living in a country house and how a 3,000 acre estate was managed. It is unlikely that the Austen family visited Godmersham anything but briefly while Thomas Knight, Edward's adoptive father, was still alive. When, after Edward's Grand Tour, he married Elizabeth Bridges, a neighbouring baronet's daughter, at Goodnestone in 1791, and lived at Rowling on the estate, the Austens did visit them there, and it was on one such visit in 1796 that Jane Austen's *Pride and Prejudice*, then called 'First Impressions', came into being. 'Are you pleased with Kent?' Darcy said, somewhat imperiously to Elizabeth Bennet.

Mr Darcy would not have wished to know that the Austen forebears, who came from Kent, had made their money through the cloth trade. Jane Austen had visited their prosperous homes in the Sevenoaks and Tonbridge area even before she made her visits to Edward in East Kent. It was while staying at Rowling that she first came to meet up with personalities such as Darcy's aunt, Lady Catherine de Bourgh of Rosings, who gave her creative ideas for lifelike grand characters and scenes. There were plenty of elegant mansions like Rosings with their great park landscapes in the neighbourhood to provide material; Chilham Castle, Eastwell Park, Godinton; and Edward's parents-in-law's, Goodnestone itself, which Jane Austen visited often, walking across the park, must have been rather intimidating after Steventon. Elizabeth Bennet, like Jane Austen herself, took such houses in her stride, whatever butterflies in her tummy her companion, Maria Lucas, might feel;

> Every park has its beauty and its prospects. Elizabeth saw much to be pleased with, though she could not be in such raptures as Mr Collins expected the scene to inspire and was but slightly affected by his enumeration of the windows in front of the house and his relations of what the glazing altogether had originally cost Sir Lewis de Bourgh.

The final inspiration for taste and high living came when Edward became possessed of a grand house himself. In 1798, four years after Thomas Knight's death,

A silhouette of the young Edward Austen being welcomed into the Knight family.

Edward's adoptive mother decided to retire to Canterbury and to allow Edward and Elizabeth Austen and their growing family to live at Godmersham. It was with the greatest of pleasure that Edward could now receive his family into his own home, and in the summer his parents and two sisters spent two months there. Jane Austen was always delighted to see him standing at the entrance 'as natural as life'. Either she or Cassandra stayed there every year to help out as yet more babies arrived.

'Living à la Godmersham' was how she learned, as she said, about 'Elegance and Ease and Luxury being above Vulgar Economy' – fires in bedrooms, carriages and coachmen, French wine and ice, late dining, ladies' maids and such niceties as knowing for which call it was appropriate to attach a flounce to your morning gown. The eldest daughter Fanny wrote to a younger sister in later years, as the rather grand Victorian Lady Knatchbull;

> Aunt Jane from various circumstances was not so refined as she ought to have been from her talent, and if she had lived 50 years later she would have been in many respects more suitable to our more refined tastes.... Both the Aunts Cassandra and Jane were brought up in a most complete ignorance of the World and its ways (I mean as to fashions etc) and if it had not been for Papa's marriage which brought them into Kent... they would have been, tho' not less clever and agreeable in themselves, very much below par as to good society and its ways.

Be that as it may, Fanny greatly enjoyed her aunt's company and confided in her as a teenager. She knew the secret of her aunt's novel-writing before it was generally known and joined in the family game of living with characters such as Darcy and Elizabeth. Edward's third daughter, Marianne, who was born in 1801, wrote;

> I remember when Aunt Jane came to us in Godmersham she used to bring the manuscript of whatever novel she was writing with her, and would shut herself up with my elder sisters in one of the bedrooms to read them aloud. I and the younger ones used to hear peals of laughter through the door and thought it very hard that we should be shut out from what was so delightful.

Jane Austen revelled in the spaciousness of Godmersham. 'Edward is gone into his woods. At this present time I have 5 tables, 28 chairs and 2 fires all to myself', she wrote to her sister. She accompanied Edward around the scattered farms on the estate and sometimes to his duties at the magistrates' court. She watched his plantations being extended and enjoyed walking up to the little Doric temple on the hill, where she could think out further plots for her novels; from it she looked out on to an Arcadian scene of grazed meadows by the little river Stour which flowed through Edward's parkland.

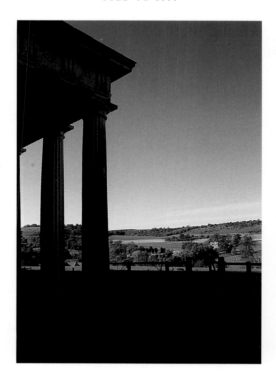

THE VIEW BACK TO THE HOUSE FROM THE DORIC TEMPLE IN WHICH JANE AUSTEN USED TO SIT.

GODMERSHAM HOUSE AND PARK.

JANE AUSTEN TOOK MANY IDEAS FOR *MANSFIELD PARK* FROM LIFE AT GODMERSHAM

The park had already been landscaped by Mr Thomas Knight as seen in the Watts engraving of 1787 and Edward, as an owner-improver, had continued, ten years later, the planting, which was 'sans peur et sans reproche' in his sister's eyes. While his adoptive mother was alive little was changed in the house but when she died in 1812, Edward decided to refurbish it throughout and to move into his other property at Chawton while this was going on. When this decision was taken Jane Austen had already begun writing *Mansfield Park*, her great country house novel, and the description of the seat as Mary Crawford contemplates it with conquest in mind, must surely be taken as one of those delightful family asides to be chuckled at out of context.

> A park, a real park 5 miles round, a spacious modern-built house, so well placed and well screened as to deserve to be in any collection of engravings of gentlemen's seats in the kingdom, and wanting only to be completely new furnished – pleasant sisters, a quiet mother and an agreeable man himself.

Bearing the circumstances in mind, we can forget Mary Crawford and the given location of Mansfield Park as 'four miles from Northampton' and imagine Mrs

GODMERSHAM DESERVED 'TO BE IN ANY COLLECTION OF ENGRAVINGS OF GENTLEMEN'S SEATS'.

Austen and her daughters looking at Godmersham in 1812, the date of the novel. The quiet mother would, of course, have caused much mirth, as the energetic, talkative Mrs Austen and the indolent Lady Bertram dozing on her sofa were complete opposites.

Having inherited the money, Edward was not only in a position to redecorate Godmersham but to take Chawton back from the tenant when the lease expired in 1812. His wife had died in 1808 after the birth of their eleventh child. Fanny, the eldest child, was only fifteen when she was called upon to help her father assume responsibility for the family and needed constant support from her aunts, Jane and Cassandra; it was at this time that Edward suggested that his mother and sisters should leave Southampton and live near him in Kent or Hampshire. They chose Chawton and moved there with great thankfulness in 1809.

Edward did not remarry and it was particularly satisfying that the Austen family could be reunited, with his mother and sisters already living in their Chawton house and James settled in their old rectory home only twelve miles away at Steventon. Edward planned to live in the 'Great House' for part of the year and make it available to his sailor brothers when on leave. He could also oblige their brother

THE NEW WALLED KITCHEN GARDEN THAT EDWARD MADE
AS SEEN TODAY.

THE AUSTENS WERE DELIGHTED WHEN EDWARD AND HIS FAMILY STAYED AT CHAWTON.
JANE AUSTEN WROTE TO HER BROTHER FRANK IN 1813, 'WE GO ON IN
THE MOST COMFORTABLE WAY, VERY FREQUENTLY DINING TOGETHER,
AND ALWAYS MEETING IN SOME PART OF EVERY DAY'.

Henry in London with shooting. 'The pleasure to us of having them here is so great, that if we were not the best creatures in the World we should not deserve it', Jane Austen wrote to her brother Frank at sea.

Mrs Austen praised Edward's 'sound judgement' and his niece Caroline, James Austen's daughter, writing reminiscences based on her mother's diary, remarked;

> My uncle Edward came to Chawton and Steventon generally twice a year to look after his affairs. He must have been more his own 'man of business' than is usual with people of large property, for I think it was his greatest interest to attend to his estates. In my recollection, he never hunted or shot.

Unlike Henry Crawford who saw Michaelmas as a time to return to his Norfolk country estate for the shooting, Edward went to Chawton and Steventon for the rent audit at that season. Like Mr Knightley, he took a great interest in the home farm when he took over Chawton, which allowed the Austens to enjoy farming activities as they had done on their glebe farm at Steventon. 'Your finding so much comfort from his Cows gave him evident pleasure', wrote Jane Austen to Cassandra.

As Chawton House had had an absentee landlord for so long, there was much scope for improvement of the grounds. It seems that Edward was already in 1811 considering re-routing a footpath through his meadows from Farringdon as Jane Austen was asked to look for an old map, which she found and sent to him. This request accounts for the details of Mr Knightley's remark to his brother;

> My idea of moving the path to Langham, of turning it more to the right that it may not cut through the home meadows, I cannot conceive any difficulty. I should not attempt it, if it were to be the means of inconvenience to the Highbury people.... The only way, of proving it, however, will be to turn to our maps'.

Edward would similarly make sure he was not inconveniencing his tenants and neighbours by the footpath diversion.

Like Mr Knightley he knew that privilege in landed estates carried responsibilities and duties not to be exploited but handed down, and we find him telling his eldest son that when he inherits, 'he is always accountable to God for the use of his possessions'. Edward's views on the vexed question of professional improvement are those voiced by the similarly high-principled Edmund Bertram in *Mansfield Park*, which was written in 1812 and 1813.

While recognising that some places needed 'a modern dress', Edmund did not want to put himself in the hands of an improver, but 'would rather have an inferior degree of beauty of my own choice, and acquired progressively' than the on-the-spot landscaping decisions of Henry Crawford in the mantle of Repton. While discussions

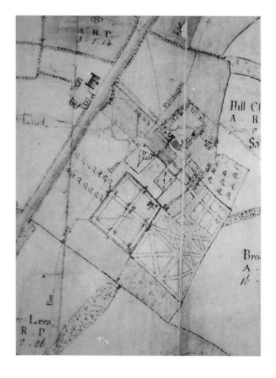

were taking place about the Chawton grounds, however, it would have been a convenient moment to borrow the Stoneleigh Red Book from Thomas Leigh to look for any appropriate ideas; however little use Edward made of the book, it would certainly give his sister many ideas for the improvement of Sotherton in *Mansfield Park*.

'Chawton is not thrown away on him', wrote Jane Austen in 1813, and in regard to his plans for the new garden, 'We like to have him proving and strengthening his attachment to the place by making it better'. Jane Austen returned with Edward to Godmersham in the autumn and admired the new decorations, particularly the Yellow Room and the Chintz Room. She had not visited for several years and enthused about the growth of Edward's plantations. Cassandra, who kept in constant touch, had been left to keep an eye on the buildings and gardening improvements at Chawton. Clearly, Edward relied on the indispensable assistance of his two sisters. He liked to have Jane by him 'to give memorandums' to and Cassandra supplied him with tapes until he bought 'a Thing for measuring Timber with' in London. On a cold March day in 1814 Edward was amazed to hear that Cassandra had planted 64 trees.

Kitchen gardens were Mrs Austen's speciality and the making of Edward's new one on the hill behind the house would have been of particular interest to her. Like Cowper, she and her daughters were ardent believers in 'snug enclosures' and able to give advice on ornamental shrubberies. When they arrived at their own Chawton home in the village in 1809 they had found two or three little enclosures with hedgerows round them which were made into a garden; as at Steventon they kept some of the existing field hedgerows and made them into shrubberies by adding ornamental shrubs, such as syringa ('for the sake of Cowper's line') and herbaceous plants to the thorns and evergreens. It was Gilpin's *Forest Scenery* that had inspired this type of garden scenery, when he pointed to Nature's shrubberies in the New Forest with their 'islands or peninsulas of forest scenery shooting into' forest lawns.

View from the terrace. The lady of the house like Miss Elliot of Kellynch took a new interest in floriculture. A seat might be brought out by a servant.

Left: A scene at Windsor Castle. Floriferous shrubberies were the order of the day for gentle exercise even at Windsor Castle. The Austens had such a walk at Steventon and at Chawton as had Mrs Grant at Mansfield rectory.

When she was writing *Mansfield Park* Jane Austen sent off an enquiry to find out if Northamptonshire, where she had sited the Bertram seat was 'a country of hedgerows' as she wanted to give Mrs Grant at the rectory such an ornamental shrubbery walk as they had in the Chawton gardens. The answer must have been in the affirmative as we find Fanny Price moralising in the Grant floriferous shrubbery *à la* Cowper;

> Every time I come into this shrubbery I am more struck with its growth and beauty. Three years ago, this was nothing but a rough hedgerow along the upper side of the field, never thought of as anything, or capable of becoming anything; and now it is converted into a walk, and it would be difficult to say whether most valuable as a convenience or an ornament; and perhaps in another three years we may be forgetting – almost forgetting what it was before.

Their Chawton shrubbery walk, in which they exercised, had also seen 'three years growth' in 1812, when Jane Austen was making Fanny Price speak as her mouthpiece. Shrubberies abound in Jane Austen's novels; Lady Bertram thinks they are the best type of improvement and even Mr Woodhouse ventures into his in perfect

THE AUSTEN COTTAGE AT CHAWTON, NOW KNOWN AS JANE AUSTEN'S HOUSE, HAS BECOME A PLACE OF LITERARY PILGRIMAGE.

weather. Mr Knightley actually proposes to Emma in the Hartfield shrubbery as they take the last turn before going in.

A delightful comment, almost certainly inserted for family amusement, is in *Persuasion*, written in 1815, when peace had finally come and Edward lent Chawton House to the returning Captain Francis Austen to the delight of his family in the cottage. When Sir Walter Elliot lets Kellynch Hall to Admiral Croft he warns his agent that he is not 'fond of the idea of my shrubberies always being approachable; and I should recommend Miss Elliot to be on her guard with respect to her flower garden'. Frank and his family, by contrast, were doubtless allowed to enjoy the Chawton garden and shrubberies to the full. What steps were taken to safeguard the furniture, however, is another matter. Whereas Mrs Croft had much in her favour because 'a lady, without a family, was the very best preserver of furniture in the world', Frank's wife arrived with five children under seven and another one was born at Chawton the following year.

THE
ROMANTIC
TIDE

———

ROMANTICS WERE CAPTIVATED BY THE SUBLIMITY
OF THE SEA. 'HE BEGAN, IN A TONE OF GREAT
TASTE AND FEELING, TO TALK OF THE SEASHORE',
WROTE JANE AUSTEN IN *SANDITON*.

115

Jane Austen's mature novels reflect the cross currents of 'Taste and Feeling' in Regency times. Her heroines, brought up with well-established Georgian standards, were caught up in the tide of new romantic ideas and a more relaxed life style. Anne Elliot in *Persuasion* was 'taught prudence in her youth, she learnt romance as she grew older'. Fanny Price in *Mansfield Park* had found that 'to sit in the shade on a fine day and look upon verdure is the most perfect refreshment'. For Anne, the 'sublimity of Nature' extended beyond Fanny's passive Cowper-inspired ideas to Lord Byron's 'boundless thoughts' on the romantic 'dark blue sea'.

The generation dilemma was apparent at Uppercross in *Persuasion*, where 'the Musgroves, like their houses, were in a state of alteration, perhaps of improvement. The father and mother were in the old English style and the young people in the new'. With their 'modern minds and manners' the 'present daughters of the house were gradually giving the proper air of confusion by a grand piano forte and a harp, flowerstands and little tables placed in every direction' at which 'the portraits themselves seemed to be staring in astonishment'. Lady Russell found the noisy activity unbearable and vowed never to call there again in the Christmas holidays.

Adapting residences to modern life, whatever the exterior style was like, was a Repton speciality. The Uppercross observations are a most telling proof that Jane Austen had studied his Stoneleigh Red Book carefully. In it Repton rejoices in the 'litter and confusion of chairs, tables, books and instruments in a modern library and living room' and condemns the 'cedar parlours occasionally mentioned in the works of Richardson where society existed without the Music, the Pamphlet or the news-papers of the present day'.

Much of 'the proper air of confusion' of the modern living room at Uppercross was caused by the young Musgrove girls chattering and 'cutting up silk and gold paper' on a side table. An 1810 essay describes the new craze for 'fancy work' clearly;

> It is impossible to congratulate our fair countrywomen too warmly on the revolution which has of late years taken place, when drawing and fancy-work of endless variety have been raised on the ruins of that heavy, unhealthy, and stupefying occupation, needlework.

The poor box of comforting garments for needy members of the parish, was not abandoned, however. Fanny Price had 'works of charity and ingenuity' on the go at the same time in her room.

While staying at Godmersham in the autumn of 1813 Jane Austen told her sailor brother Frank in a letter that Fanny had gone to a fair and would bring back all the gold paper that everybody in the family would need for the year. This would be of particular interest to Frank who was the Austen handyman-craftsman; we hear of

A PAGE FROM REPTON'S *FRAGMENTS ON THE THEORY AND PRACTICE OF LANDSCAPE GARDENING*, 1816, SHOWING HOW TO IMPROVE THE GLOOM OF THE OLD-FASHIONED CEDAR PARLOUR AS DESCRIBED IN THE RED BOOK FOR STONELEIGH.

INTERIORS

him making curtain fringes for the house they had shared at Southampton. He made toys for the children and trinkets for presents, which included little ivory boxes decorated with gold medallions, for which Fanny's purchase of gold foil embossed borders would be of interest. Frank would not have been accused of 'wasting gold paper' as were the young Bertram girls in *Mansfield Park*. Captain Harville in *Persuasion* had the same dexterity with his fingers, which he put to good use when he was invalided out of the navy, drawing and making toys and nets, varnishing and carpentry. In later years Frank Austen suggested that he thought that parts of Captain Harville's character 'were drawn from myself. At least some of his domestic habits, tastes and occupations bear a strong resemblance to mine'.

One of the most exciting forms of fancy work, introduced in 1796, was the transparency, made by colouring and varnishing the back of a print to give it translucency when held up to the light; the effect, with internal views of gothic abbeys, moonlit scenes and torch-bearing banditti in caves, was both picturesque and romantic. Jane Austen admired those she saw at Mrs Branston's house at Oakley Hall, near Steventon, in 1800. Fanny Price inherited the old schoolroom at Mansfield Park which still had transparencies fixed on the three lower panes of the window, which had been made by the young Bertram girls, when the rage was at its height; 'Tintern Abbey held its station between a cave in Italy and a moonlight lake in Cumberland'.

Regency costume perfectly expressed the new relaxed style of living. Gone was the upholstered look with quilted petticoats and hoops and boned bodices. The new craze for playing the harp allowed a seated elegant figure in a clinging high-waisted, low necked dress with graceful folds of the skirt, to be shown to great advantage; the soulful tones and romantic tradition of the instrument were particularly beguiling. Mary Crawford was anxious to get her harp sent down from London to Mansfield rectory so that she could with her 'greatest obligingness' play it to Edmund Bertram with 'an expression and taste which were peculiarly becoming'. The ruse succeeded as Edmund called in every day to be 'indulged with his favourite instrument' and 'every thing was soon in a fair train'.

The playful, detached general remark that follows this episode was probably inserted for the benefit of Fanny Knight, who was in the throes of an uncertain love affair and talked of learning to play the harp;

> A young woman, pretty, lively, with a harp as elegant as herself; and both placed near a window, cut down to the ground, and opening on a little lawn, surrounded by shrubs in the rich foliage of summer, was enough to catch any man's heart.

Persuasion, not written until 1815, catches the relaxed mood of the country in terms of architecture as well as fashion and lifestyle. Regency taste was more flexible

TWO TRANSPARENCIES OF THE KIND THAT
WERE FIXED ON THE THREE LOWER PANES
OF THE WINDOWS OF THE SCHOOLROOM AT
MANSFIELD PARK AND HAD BEEN MADE
BY THE BERTRAM GIRLS WHEN THE
RAGE WAS AT ITS HEIGHT.

and intuitive than the Georgian had been and it embraced a wider and more democratic society. In place of Palladian stairways, pediments and porticoes, Regency houses had striped canopies, verandahs, balconies and ornamental ironwork. The village of Uppercross in *Persuasion* was 'completely in the old English style containing only two houses superior in appearance to those of the yeomen and labourers', the mansion and the parsonage. When the squire's son, Charles Musgrove, married Mary Elliot, however, 'it had received the improvement of a farm-house elevated into a cottage for his residence; and Uppercross Cottage, with its viranda, French windows, and other prettinesses' was likely to be the first place to catch the traveller's eye.

Dr Johnson's *Dictionary* defined cottages as 'mean habitations', but by the time Jane Austen was writing they had become models for genteel residences. The dandyish Robert Ferrars in *Sense and Sensibility* was;

> excessively fond of a cottage; there is always so much comfort, so much elegance about them... I advise everybody who is going to build, to build a cottage. My friend Lord Courtland came to me the other day on purpose to ask my advice, and laid before me three different plans of Bonomi's. I was to decide the best of them. 'My dear Courtland', said I, immediately throwing them all in the fire, 'do not adopt either of them, but by all means build a cottage'. And that, I fancy will be the end of it.

Jane Austen would have known Bonomi's work with his monumental porticoes at Eastwell Park, near Godmersham and Laverstoke Park, near Steventon.

Robert Ferrars then went on to give his ideas about rearranging the cottage room for genteel supper parties and card tables as required. 'So that, in fact, you see, if people do but know how to set about it, every comfort may be as well enjoyed in a cottage as in the most spacious dwelling'. This cottage cult implied Feeling, which the romantically-inclined thought to be better than Taste, but it was a far cry from the genuine cottage life style with Oliver Goldsmith's 'calm desires that need but little room'.

These gentlemen's retreats were often in the nature of fishing lodges or shooting-boxes and had stables and out-buildings, but an increasing number became main residences. The term *cottage orné* for such a cottage-style affluent dwelling seems to have been coined by Robert Lugar in 1805. Jane Austen uses it once in her unfinished seaside novel *Sanditon*, which she began to write in 1817. The Austens sometimes referred to their Chawton house as 'the cottage' to distinguish it from the 'Great House', but it was never referred to as Chawton Cottage, as it is today.

Thomas Love Peacock highlights the new trend for living in a *cottage orné* without estate responsibilities or thought of posterity. An old man in *Melincourt*, published in 1818, describes how the squire, beloved of his tenantry, was forced to leave

BELOW: THE MODERN LIVING ROOM AT UPPERCROSS IN *PERSUASION* WAS IN THE PROCESS OF ACQUIRING 'THE PROPER AIR OF CONFUSION'.

RIGHT: 'A YOUNG WOMAN, PRETTY,
LIVELY, WITH A HARP AS ELEGANT
AS HERSELF... WAS ENOUGH TO
CATCH ANY MAN'S HEART'.
EDMUND BERTRAM SUCCUMBED
READILY ENOUGH.

OVERLEAF: KNOWLE COTTAGE,
SIDMOUTH. A FINE *COTTAGE ORNÉ*
DEMONSTRATING THE RELAXED
STYLE OF LIVING FAVOURED IN
REGENCY TIMES. JANE AUSTEN
VISITED SIDMOUTH IN 1801.

the mansion house through taxes and 'paper money' and how the estate was broken up into plots;

> Every now and then came a queer zort of chap dropped out o' the sky like – a vundholder he called un – and bought a bit of ground vor a handvul of paper and built a cottage horny, as they call it – there be one of these on the hill-zide – and had nothing to do wi' the country people, nor the country people wi' he: nothing in the world to do, as we could zee, but to eat and drink, and make little bits of shrubberies, o' quashies, and brutuses, and zalies and cubies and filigrees and ruddydunderums, instead of the oak plantations the old landlords used to plant.

Mary Crawford's uncle, Admiral Crawford, bought a summer cottage in Twickenham, after the great Twickenham Park estate had been broken up in 1805. This was presumably bought with prize money rather than what Repton called the 'upstart wealth' of the new industrialists and speculators. The cottage was 'excessively pretty' and was improved with shrubberies, a gravel walk and rustic seats, but when the admiral installed his mistress there, Mary Crawford was forced to leave and take refuge with her half-sister at Mansfield rectory.

Twickenham is thus given a bad name by Jane Austen. It had a tradition of ease of social communication between an unique out-of-town cultural set consisting of aristocrats, poets, actors, painters and musicians who had the freedom of each other's gardens, libraries and harpsichords; this allowed Henry Crawford, who was staying at nearby Richmond, to turn up at any time at the house where Mrs Rushworth was living with friends, which resulted in their elopement and disgrace to Mansfield Park.

There was a move for the nouveaux riches to build new villa-type houses on the fringe of towns. Jane Austen comments on this in her unpublished 'The Watsons', written in 1803. In 'the town of D in Surrey', thought to be Dorking, she tells us that Mr Edwards lived in the main street in a grand house whose door was opened by 'a man in livery with a powdered head' and adds that it was 'the best in the place, if Mr Tomlinson the banker might be indulged in calling his newly erected house at the end of the town with a shrubbery and a sweep in the country'.

Hartfield, the Woodhouses' residence in *Emma*, poses problems in terms of out-of-town social structure. We are told that it was 'modern and well-built' and 'in spite of its separate lawn and shrubberies' and small private grounds it did 'really belong' to the 'large and populous village, almost amounting to a town' called Highbury. There is no suggestion of a nouveau-riche background; indeed Mr Woodhouse, who prides himself on his good breeding, is a most unlikely entrepreneur; and we are told at the beginning of *Emma* that the Woodhouses were 'first

in consequence' in Highbury and that 'all looked up to them', which is increasingly apparent as the novel proceeds.

The insufferable Mrs Elton, newly-arrived in Highbury, finds that her brother-in-law's place, Maple Grove, just outside Bristol, is 'extremely like' Hartfield, much to the annoyance of Emma Woodhouse. She refers to Maple Grove as, 'My brother Mr Suckling's seat', but Maple Grove was clearly no more of a 'seat' than Hartfield. Jane Austen had stayed at Clifton, the Bristol suburb of elegant town houses, in 1806, and would have seen that wealthy Bristol businessmen were seeking their own plots of land for building further away from the city in a desire for privacy and natural sur-roundings. Maple Grove, 'very retired' behind its shrubberies, was probably situated at the edge of one of the nearest villages, such as Redland, near enough to go 'explor-ing' Kings Weston in their famous barouche-landau. The Sucklings had lived there for eleven years and Mrs Elton, who had 'quite a horror of upstarts', deplored some lately-arrived neighbours, who had made their money in Birmingham, 'giving themselves immense airs, and expecting to be on a footing with the old established families'.

The newest and most romantic social change was the cult of seaside retire-ment combined with sea bathing, which Jane Austen highlights in her unfinished novel *Sanditon*. The Prince of Wales popularised the idea when he took up residence

A *COTTAGE ORNÉ* IN WINDSOR FOREST WITH SHRUBBERIES FLOUNCED AMID MATURE TREES.

RIGHT: 'MORNING AMUSEMENTS AT BRIGHTON'. LYDIA SET HER HEART ON BRIGHTON, BUT JANE AUSTEN HAD A HORROR OF IT.

TURNER DESIGNED THIS ORNAMENTAL
VILLA IN TWICKENHAM FOR HIMSELF IN
1810. ADMIRAL CRAWFORD ACQUIRED
SUCH A VILLA IN *MANSFIELD PARK*

in Brighton in 1786 in a modest little farmhouse with only a few shrubs and roses shutting it off from the road; this would later become the most fantastic of all seaside extravaganzas, the exotic Royal Pavilion. Dr Richard Russell had promoted the health-giving properties of drinking sea water and bathing. Brighton was near to London and soon came to rival the inland spas of Bath and Tunbridge Wells. Even Dr Johnson was tempted to breathe its ozone, if not actually to bathe.

There were other attractions besides the sea air, as Lydia Bennet knew full well when she tried to persuade her father that 'a little sea-bathing would set me up for ever'. Brighton was then full of officers with 'all the glories of the camp'. Brighton was nothing if not smart and vulgar; by 1796 the sixth edition of *The New Brighton Guide* could advertise it as a place 'where the sinews of morality are so happily relaxed, that a bawd and a baroness may snore in the same tenement'. Jane Austen wanted none of it herself and wrote to her sister in 1799; 'I assure you that I dread the idea of going to Brighton as much as you do, but I am not without hopes that something may happen to prevent it'.

There is no record of a dreaded Brighton visit, but Jane Austen did enjoy more select seaside holidays with her parents when living in Bath; at Sidmouth in 1801; Dawlish in 1802 and at Lyme in 1803 and 1804. In 1805, after Mr Austen's death, Edward arranged for a family holiday at Worthing. The Austens seemed undeterred that there were then plans to evacuate the coast, following new threats of invasion. Fanny Knight's diary gives 17 September 1805 as the date of their party leaving Godmersham and noted the next day;

> I went with G. Mamma in the morning to buy fish on the beach and afterwards with Mamma and Miss Sharpe to Bathe where I had a most delicious dip.... We dined at 4 and went to a Raffle in the evening where Aunt Jane won and it amounted to 18/- d.

Fanny and her parents only stayed a short while, but the Austens and Martha Lloyd stayed on until November, possibly being joined by Henry and Eliza, and may have remained there over Christmas.

Edward would have taken a house for the period and brought servants with him. Crabs and lobsters and all the novelty of fresh fish would have delighted Mrs Austen, who clearly wanted to do the buying herself. 'Saline air and immersion', as recommended by Mr Parker of *Sanditon*, were the order of the day. Jane Austen enjoyed bathing even in November, but there is no mention of Mrs Austen taking part in 'dipping'.

Worthing, however, was not the Sanditon of Jane Austen's novel; it had grown piecemeal from a little village after the Princess Amelia was sent there to recuperate in 1798. Sanditon was a purpose-built seaside resort put up by an entrepreneur. The only such Sussex resort on which it could have been modelled was Bognor, formerly called Hothamton after its founder Sir Richard Hotham, who saw himself as both entrepreneur and benefactor and had invested £60,000 in the seaside project, which was, like Mr Parker's, 'his hobby horse, his occupation, his hope and his futurity'.

Jane Austen could have read about Bognor in the *Sussex Weekly Advertiser* while at Worthing or in the national newspapers and magazines. She may even have visited it. By 1807 the Bognor guide claimed that 'there was no spot on the coast of England better calculated for the two-fold purpose of sea-bathing and retirement'. While the Austens were at Worthing news of Trafalgar came through, which would have been a great relief to them as Frank was on the *Canopus* in the Mediterranean. Nelson's victory removed the threat of invasion and Trafalgar immediately became a popular name for new houses. When Jane Austen came to write *Sanditon* in 1817, however, 'Waterloo is more the thing now', in the words of Mr Parker, Sanditon's 'projector', who had called his home Trafalgar House, and now hoped to name a little crescent to commemorate Waterloo.

TURNER'S WATERCOLOUR PAINTING OF LYME REGIS FROM CHARMOUTH.
JANE AUSTEN LOVED LYME REGIS WHERE SHE STAYED IN 1803 AND 1804 AND IT WAS HERE THAT ANNE ELLIOT
DISCUSSED ROMANTIC POETRY WITH CAPTAIN BENWICK.

The purpose of building the resort of Bognor had been, like that of Sanditon, to attract high class clients who shunned the rowdyism of Brighton and the larger resorts. Even the *Evangelical Magazine* commended it as a place where its readers could enjoy sea-bathing without fear of 'dissipations'. Like Sanditon, it had a hotel, a subscription room and library, a milliner's shop, a warm bath and bathing machines. It was clearly no place to attract Lydia Bennet but may well have been the goal of the Knightleys who spent their honeymoon on the coast within convenient distance of their Surrey home.

Jane Austen saw speculative ventures, profit making and alluring advertising as a challenge to traditional ways of life. She also disliked the idea of exploiting hypochondria. Mr Parker is not portrayed as vicious, however, only misguided. We do not know if Sanditon was to fail and Mr Parker find himself heavily in debt, as happened to Sir Richard Hotham. If Trafalgar House had had to be sold Mrs Parker would undoubtedly have rejoiced to return to her sheltered old house, a mile and three quarters inland. She would also have enjoyed having back her nice garden and orchard, but particularly the self-sufficiency of her kitchen garden after having to buy in her vegetable produce in the new Sanditon. Mrs Austen would have thoroughly approved of the reclamation of the kitchen garden and Mr Parker would have had to resign himself once again to 'the yearly nuisance of its decaying vegetation'.

Sir Edward Denham, the nephew of Lady Denham, Mr Parker's 'colleague in speculation' was aware that the romantic poets were giving a great boost to the cult of the sea. 'He began, in a tone of great taste and feeling, to talk of the sea and the seashore'. Scott's beautiful lines were apparently never out of his mind at Sanditon. The bewildered heroine, Charlotte Heywood, could not recall any remarks by Scott on the sea; it was of course Byron's sea Sir Edward was searching for; 'Dark-heaving - boundless, endless and sublime – The Image of Eternity'.

Jane Austen had already enjoyed the sublimity of the sea before Byron eulogised it in *Childe Harold* in 1812. The *Memoir* recalled the delight she had in watching the ebb and flow of the tide, as did Anne Elliot, at Charmouth, in 'unwearied contemplation'. She took long walks on the cliffs at Lyme and in *Persuasion* lovingly describes the landslip of 'Pinny with its green chasms between romantic rocks'; with a most unusual intrusion of her own sentiments she observes, 'A very strange stranger it must be who does not see charms in the immediate environs of Lyme, to make her wish to know it better'. Her rambles at Lyme were taken in the company of her favourite brother Henry, which would have added to her pleasure.

It is following Jane Austen's eulogy of the Lyme landscape in *Persuasion* that Anne Elliot discusses romantic poetry with Captain Benwick. They talked of 'the richness of the present age' and tried to 'ascertain whether "Marmion"' or "The Lady of the Lake" were to be preferred, and how ranked "The Giaour" and "The Bride of Abydos"; and moreover how "The Giaour" was to be pronounced'. Captain Benwick, whose fiancée had recently died, was 'acquainted with all the tenderest songs of the one poet, and all the impassioned descriptions of hopeless agony of the other'. Scott's poetry we know gave Jane Austen great pleasure, but her only comment on Byron is in a letter to her sister in 1814, when she says, nonchalantly, 'I have read the Corsair, mended my petticoat and have nothing else to do'.

Eighteenth-century sensibility had changed into romantic agony and Jane Austen was only prepared to go so far with it. Anne Elliot gently warned Captain Benwick that she thought 'it was the misfortune of poetry, to be seldom safely enjoyed by those who enjoyed it completely' and 'recommended a larger allowance of prose in his daily study'. Cowper's *Letters*, which showed his religious consolation in overcoming depression, would have been on her mind. There was little comfort for uneasy hearts in Byron, whose romantic heroes learned 'to love despair'.

Jane Austen had little time for the socialist propaganda of William Godwin and remarked of someone she met in Bath that he was as 'raffish in his appearance as I would wish every Disciple of Godwin to be'. Her views on enlightened peasantry and political justice were probably expressed by Emma Woodhouse, who had 'no romantic expectations of extraordinary virtue from those for whom education had done so little'. She was, however, a great admirer of George Crabbe's truth to nature and concern for the common man, and laughingly said that if she married at all she could fancy being Mrs Crabbe. She named a heroine after the poet's entry in his *The Parish Register* – the 'chaste' Fanny Price, who was found by Edmund reading Crabbe's *Tales*, recently published in 1812, in her sanctuary.

Henry Austen affirmed that his sister 'seldom changed her views on books and men'; with Crabbe's humane realism, Cowper's morals and sincere praise of Nature, 'not conjured up to serve occasions of poetic pomp', and Gilpin's guidance on matters of taste she could reconcile the old and the new to her own satisfaction.

Table of dates
in the life of Jane Austen and comparative literary landmarks

1775 Birth at Steventon rectory
1785-87 Abbey School, Reading
1789-90 James and Henry Austen edit *The Loiterer* at Oxford
1787-90 *Frederica and Elfrida, Henry and Eliza* and other
  youthful compositions
1790 *Love and Freindship*
1791 *The History of England* with Cassandra's illustrations
1792 *Lesley Castle*
     Catherine or the Bower
1795 'Elinor and Marianne' (subsequently *Sense and Sensibility*)
1796 'First Impressions' (subsequently *Pride and Prejudice*)
1797 *Northanger Abbey* (originally called 'Susan') begun
     'First Impressions' rejected by Cadell
1798 Edward's widowed adoptive mother, Mrs Knight, leaves
  Godmersham; he and his wife move in. Austen family visit.
1799 Visit to Bath
1801 Removal from Steventon to Bath
     Holiday at Sidmouth
1802 Holiday at Dawlish
1803 Holiday at Lyme
     Unfinished novel *The Watsons* begun
     Northanger Abbey, advertised as 'Susan', sold to Crosby
1804 Return to Lyme for holiday
1805 Death of Revd George Austen at Bath
     Autumn family holiday at Worthing arranged by Edward
1806 Removal of family from Bath to Southampton with summer
  visits to Adlestrop, Stoneleigh Abbey and Hamstall Ridware
1809 Removal with family from Southampton to Chawton
     James and family at Stoneleigh Abbey
     Presentation of Red Book on Stoneleigh Abbey by Repton
     Attempt to secure publication of *Northanger Abbey*
1811 *Sense and Sensibility* published by Egerton
     Mansfield Park begun
1812 Mrs Knight dies; Edward inherits all the Knight property and
  takes back Chawton House
1813 *Pride and Prejudice* published by Egerton
     Knights at Chawton for the summer
1814 *Mansfield Park* published by Egerton
     At Great Bookham with the Cookes
     Emma begun
1815 *Persuasion* begun and completed the following year
     Emma published by John Murray
1817 Unfinished draft of *Sanditon* written
     Death in Winchester and burial in the cathedral
1818 *Northanger Abbey* and *Persuasion* published posthumously with
  biographical preface by Henry Austen
1870 A Memoir of Jane Austen published by James Edward Austen-Leigh,
  Jane Austen's nephew

1742 Edward Young, *Night Thoughts*
1743 Robert Blair *The Grave*
1747 Thomas Warton, *The Pleasures of Melancholy*
1753 Samuel Richardson, *Sir Charles Grandison*
     William Hogarth, *Analysis of Beauty*
1757 Edmund Burke, *Philosophical Enquiry*
     Thomas Gray, *The Bard*
1761 J.J.Rousseau, *Julie, ou La Nouvelle Héloïse*
1762 James Macpherson (Ossian), *Fingal, an ancient epic poem*
1764 Horace Walpole, *Castle of Otranto*
1768 William Gilpin, *Essay on Prints*
1774 J.W.Goethe, *The Sorrows of Werther*
1778 Fanny Burney, *Evelina*
1782 William Gilpin, *Wye Tour*
1784 Charlotte Smith, *Elegiac Sonnets*
1785 William Cowper, *The Task*
1786 William Gilpin, *Lakes Tour*
     Charlotte Smith, *Emmeline*
1789 William Gilpin, *Highlands Tour*
     Gilbert White, *The Natural History of Selborne*
     Charlotte Smith, *Ethelinde*
1791 William Gilpin, *Forest Scenery*
     Anne Radcliffe, *Romance of the Forest*
1793 French Revolutionary Wars
1793 William Godwin, *Enquiry concerning Political Justice*
     Charlotte Smith, *The Old Manor House*
1794 Anne Radcliffe, *The Mysteries of Udolpho*
     Uvedale Price, *Essay on the Picturesque*
     Richard Payne Knight, *The Landscape*
1796 Fanny Burney, *Camilla*
     M.G.Lewis, *The Monk*
1798 *Lyrical Ballads*: Poems by Wordsworth and Coleridge
1801 Uvedal Price, *Dialogue on the distinct Characters*
  of the Picturesque and the Beautiful
     M.G.Lewis, *Tales of Wonder*
1803 Humphry Repton, *Observations on the Theory*
  and Practice of Landscape Gardening
     William Hayley, *Life and Letters of William Cowper*
1805 Walter Scott, *The Lay of the Last Minstrel*
1805 Battle of Trafalgar
1807 George Crabbe, *The Parish Register*
1808 Walter Scott, *Marmion*
1810 Walter Scott, *The Lady of the Lake*
1812 George Crabbe, *Tales in Verse*
     Lord Byron, *Childe Harold*
     William Combe, *Tour of Dr Syntax in search of the Picturesque*
     J.C.Loudon, *Observations on laying out Farms in the Scotch style*
1813 Lord Byron, *The Bride of Abydos*
     Lord Byron, *The Corsair*
     Lord Byron, *The Giaour*
1814 Walter Scott, *Waverley*
1815 Battle of Waterloo. Peace in Europe

Acknowledgements
I am particularly grateful to George Carter, Christopher Dingwall, Hazel Fryer, Keith Goodway, Peter Hayden, Cassie Knight, David Lambert, Kedrun Laurie, Dodie Masterman, Wendy Osborne, Stella Palmer, Michael Symes, Eileen Stamers-Smith, Nigel Temple, Sybil Wade, Elisabeth Whittle and Kim Wilkie.

My chief thanks are to my husband, who shares my enthusiasm for Jane Austen and her works and has given me much help and encouragement in writing this book.

The publishers would like to thank Pippa Gatward, Richard Crawley and Rosemary Smith for their help and advice.